# BUSTED

## CHORD SONGBOOK

*Fifteen songs with complete lyrics, guitar chord boxes and chord symbols.*

## HOW TO USE THIS BOOK

All the songs in this book have been carefully arranged to sound great on the acoustic guitar. T are in the same keys as the original recordings, and where possible authentic chord voicings h been used, except where an alternative voicing more accurately reflects the overall tonality.

Where a capo was used on the original track, it is indicated at the top of the song under the ch boxes. If you don't have a capo, you can still play the song, but it won't sound in the same key as original. Where a song is played in an altered tuning, that is also indicated at the top of the son

## UNDERSTANDING CHORD BOXES

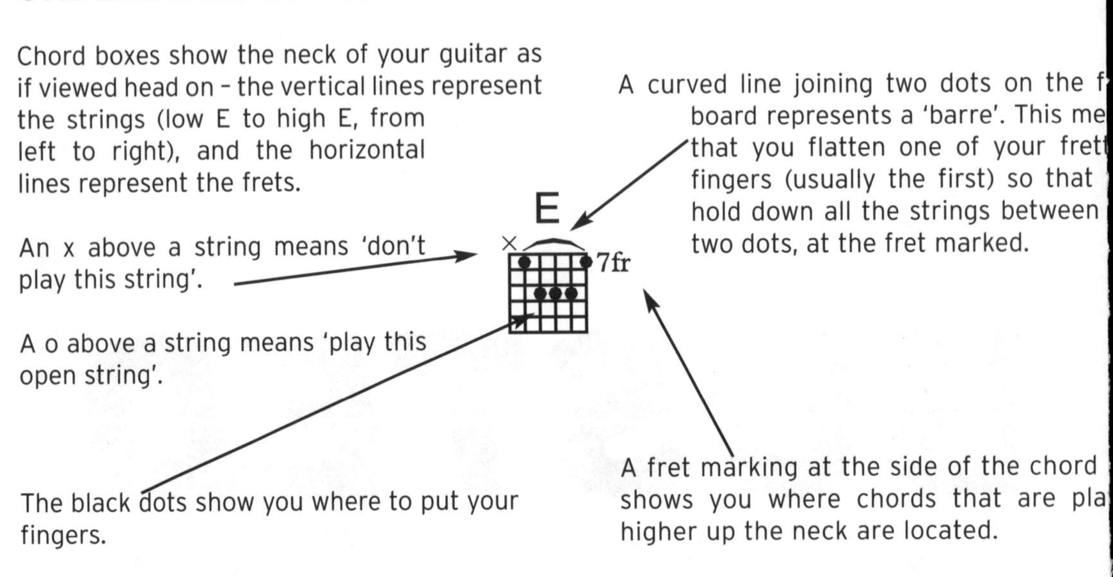


Chord boxes show the neck of your guitar as if viewed head on – the vertical lines represent the strings (low E to high E, from left to right), and the horizontal lines represent the frets.

An x above a string means 'don't play this string'.

A o above a string means 'play this open string'.

The black dots show you where to put your fingers.

A curved line joining two dots on the f board represents a 'barre'. This me that you flatten one of your fret fingers (usually the first) so that hold down all the strings between two dots, at the fret marked.

A fret marking at the side of the chord shows you where chords that are pla higher up the neck are located.

## TUNING YOUR GUITAR

The best way to tune your guitar is to use an electronic tuner. Alternatively, you can relative tuning – this will ensure that your guitar is in tune with itself, but won't guaran that you will be in tune with the original track (or any other musicians).

## HOW TO USE RELATIVE TUNING

Fret the low E string at the 5th fret and pluck – compare this with the sound of the open A strir The two notes should be in tune – if not, adjust the tuning of the A string until the two notes mat

Repeat this process for the other strings according to this diagram:

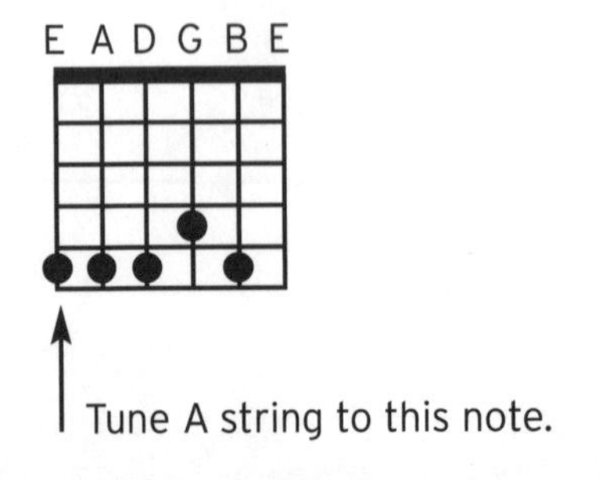


Note that the B string should match the note the 4th fret of the G string, whereas all the oth strings match the note at the 5th fret of t string below.

As a final check, ensure that the bottom E stri and top E string are in tune with each other.

# CONTENTS



*Published 2004*

*Griffin House 161 Hammersmith Road London England W6 8BS*

*Editorial, arranging and engraving by Artemis Music Limited*
*(www.artemismusic.com)*

# 3AM

*Words and Music by*
*CHARLIE SIMPSON, JAMES BOURNE, MATHEW SARGEANT,*
*LAUREN CHRISTY, SCOTT SPOCK* AND *GRAHAM EDWARDS*

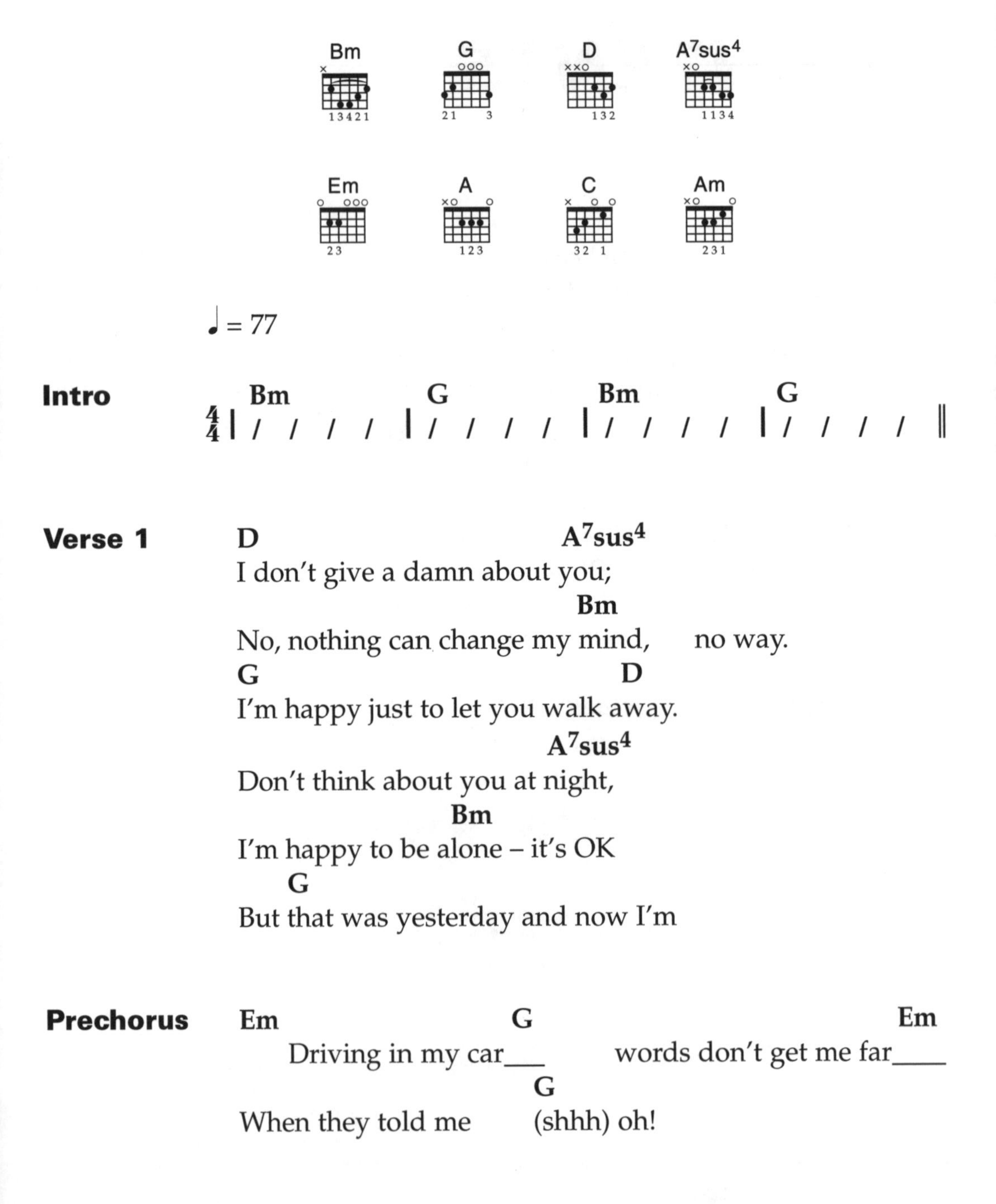


**Intro** 4/4 | **Bm** / / / / | **G** / / / / | **Bm** / / / / | **G** / / / / ||

**Verse 1**

```
D                                A7sus4
I don't give a damn about you;
                                  Bm
No, nothing can change my mind,      no way.
G                                     D
I'm happy just to let you walk away.
                               A7sus4
Don't think about you at night,
                        Bm
I'm happy to be alone – it's OK
    G
But that was yesterday and now I'm
```

**Prechorus**

```
Em                  G                        Em
    Driving in my car___     words don't get me far____
                         G
When they told me        (shhh) oh!
```

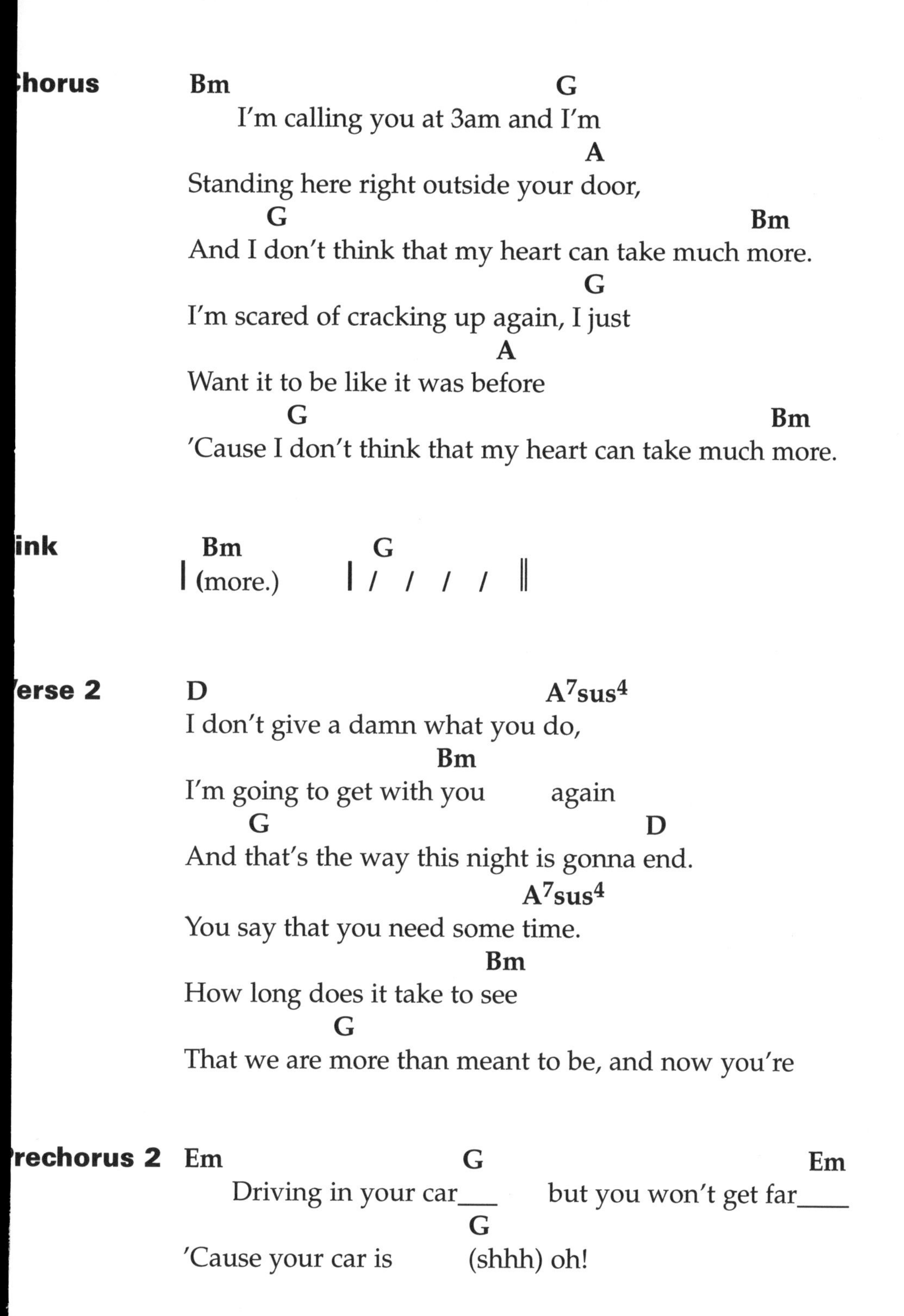

**[C]horus**

Bm G
I'm calling you at 3am and I'm
A
Standing here right outside your door,
G Bm
And I don't think that my heart can take much more.
G
I'm scared of cracking up again, I just
A
Want it to be like it was before
G Bm
'Cause I don't think that my heart can take much more.

**[L]ink**

Bm G
| (more.) | / / / / ||

**[V]erse 2**

D $A^7sus^4$
I don't give a damn what you do,
Bm
I'm going to get with you again
G D
And that's the way this night is gonna end.
$A^7sus^4$
You say that you need some time.
Bm
How long does it take to see
G
That we are more than meant to be, and now you're

**[P]rechorus 2**

Em G Em
Driving in your car___ but you won't get far___
G
'Cause your car is (shhh) oh!

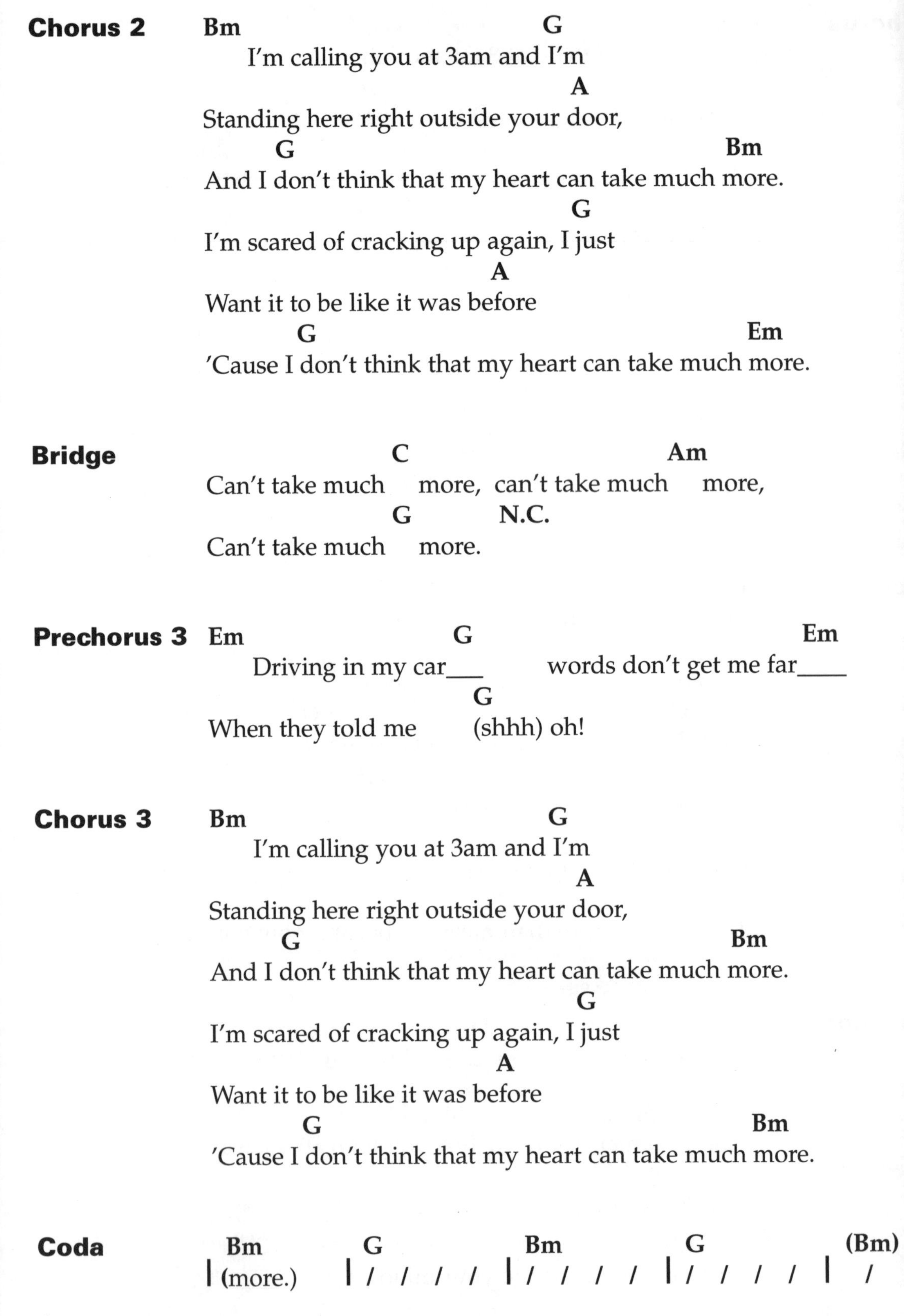

**Chorus 2**

Bm G
I'm calling you at 3am and I'm
A
Standing here right outside your door,
G Bm
And I don't think that my heart can take much more.
G
I'm scared of cracking up again, I just
A
Want it to be like it was before
G Em
'Cause I don't think that my heart can take much more.

**Bridge**

C Am
Can't take much more, can't take much more,
G N.C.
Can't take much more.

**Prechorus 3**

Em G Em
Driving in my car___ words don't get me far____
G
When they told me (shhh) oh!

**Chorus 3**

Bm G
I'm calling you at 3am and I'm
A
Standing here right outside your door,
G Bm
And I don't think that my heart can take much more.
G
I'm scared of cracking up again, I just
A
Want it to be like it was before
G Bm
'Cause I don't think that my heart can take much more.

**Coda**

Bm G Bm G (Bm)
| (more.) | / / / / | / / / / | / / / / | / ||

# ALL THE WAY

Words and Music by
JAMES BOURNE, MATHEW SARGEANT,
AND CHARLIE SIMPSON

G D/F# C(9) Em D A7sus4

**Capo 2nd fret**

♩ = 170

**tro**

G D/F# C(9)
4/4 ||: / / / / | / / / / | / / / / | / / / / :||

**erse 1**

G D/F#
It happens every time, you've given me the sign,
Em D C(9)
We start to get it on but then you stop me.
G D/F#
You know I've had it up to here, you need to be more clear,
Em D
'Cause you're the one that led me here,
C(9) D
So take me.

**horus**

G D
'Cause you said that you would but then you changed your mind.
A7sus4
How could you do this to me?
C(9) D
It's just so unkind.
G D
And it's cruel if you say that you'll go all the way,
A7sus4
I can't wait for the day
C(9) D G D C(9) D
That you don't change your mind.___________

**Verse 2**

G D/F♯
You've got to understand things are getting out of hand.
Em D $C^{(9)}$
You can't just leave me sitting here unseen to.
G
You know I don't know what to do,
D/F♯
Or how long to wait for you,
Em D $C^{(9)}$ D
You said you needed time so I won't rush you.

**Chorus 2**

G D
'Cause you said that you would but then you changed your mind
$A^7sus^4$
How could you do this to me?
$C^{(9)}$ D
It's just so unkind.
G D
And it's cruel if you say that you'll go all the way,
$A^7sus^4$
I can't wait for the day
$C^{(9)}$ D G D $C^{(9)}$
That you don't change your mind.___________
D G D $C^{(9)}$ D
That you don't change your mind.___________

**Bridge**

Em D/F♯ $C^{(9)}$
I'll never let you down, I'll always be around,

When you need someone
D Em
To catch you when you fall down.
D $C^{(9)}$
I'm waiting here for you if you decide you want to.
G
If you want me to stay
D/F♯ $C^{(9)}$ D
Then I'm only a phone call away.

**horus 3**

G N.C. D N.C.
'Cause you said that you would but then you changed your mind.
A7sus4 N.C.
How could you do this to me?
C(9) D
It's just so unkind.
G D
And it's cruel if you say that you'll go all the way,
A7sus4 C(9)
I can't wait for the day that you don't change.

**horus 4**

G D
And it's cruel if you say that you'll go all the way,
A7sus4
I can't wait for the day
C(9) G D C(9)
That you don't change your mind,____________
D N.C.
You don't change your mind. ‖

# AIR HOSTESS

*Words and Music by*
*JAMES BOURNE, TOM FLETCHER,*
*MATHEW SARGEANT AND CHARLIE SIMPSON*

D　$A^7sus^4$　$Em^7$　G　A　$Gmaj^7$

♩ = 185

**Intro**

(D)
4/4 | / / / / | / / / / | / / / / |

(D)　　　　　　D
(Let's go!) | / / / / | / / / / |

$A^7sus^4$　$Em^7$　　　D　G
(Yeah! Alright!) | / / / / | / / / / | / / / / ||

**Verse 1**

D
Walking through the terminal
A
I saw something beautiful:
$Em^7$　　　　　　$Gmaj^7$
You left for your duty call.______
D
Next I'm getting on the plane,
A
That's when I see you again.
$Em^7$　　　　　　$Gmaj^7$
I can't get you off my brain______ (let's go!)

**echorus**

**Em7**
That uniform you're wearing
**G**
So hot I can't stop staring,
**D** **A**
You're putting on an awesome show.
**Em7**
The cabin pressure's rising,
**G** **A7sus4** **A**
My coke has got no ice in there.______

**horus**

**D** **A7sus4**
Air hostess, I like the way you dress.
**Em7** **D**
You know I hate to fly but I feel much better,
**G**
Occupied my mind writing you a love-letter,
**D** **A7sus4**
I messed my pants when we flew over France.
**Em7**
Will I see you soon in my hotel room
**D** **G** **A**
For a holiday romance?
**N.C.** **G**
Air hostess.

**erse 2**

**D**
Throwing peanuts down the aisle –
**A**
Stupid, but it made you smile –
**Em7** **Gmaj7**
You came over for a while.______
**D**
Then you whispered in my ear
**A**
The words that I longed to hear
**Em7** **Gmaj7**
"I want you to thrill me here."______

**Prechorus 2**

Em$^{7}$ G
You can't because you're working, the paparazzi's lurkin
D A
You didn't know I'm in a band.
Em$^{7}$ G
In England people know me,
A$^{7}$sus$^{4}$ A
One photo's worth a hundred grand.______

**Chorus 2**

D A$^{7}$sus$^{4}$
Air hostess, I like the way you dress.
Em$^{7}$ D
You know I hate to fly but I feel much better,
G
Occupied my mind writing you a love-letter,
D A$^{7}$sus$^{4}$
I messed my pants when we flew over France.
Em$^{7}$
Will I see you soon in my hotel room
D G A
For a holiday romance?
N.C. G
Air hostess.

**Bridge**

D A Em$^{7}$
Na, na na-na, na, na na-na.
G A D
Na, na na-na, na, na na-na.
A Em$^{7}$
Na, na na-na, na, na na-na.
G A
Na, na na-na.

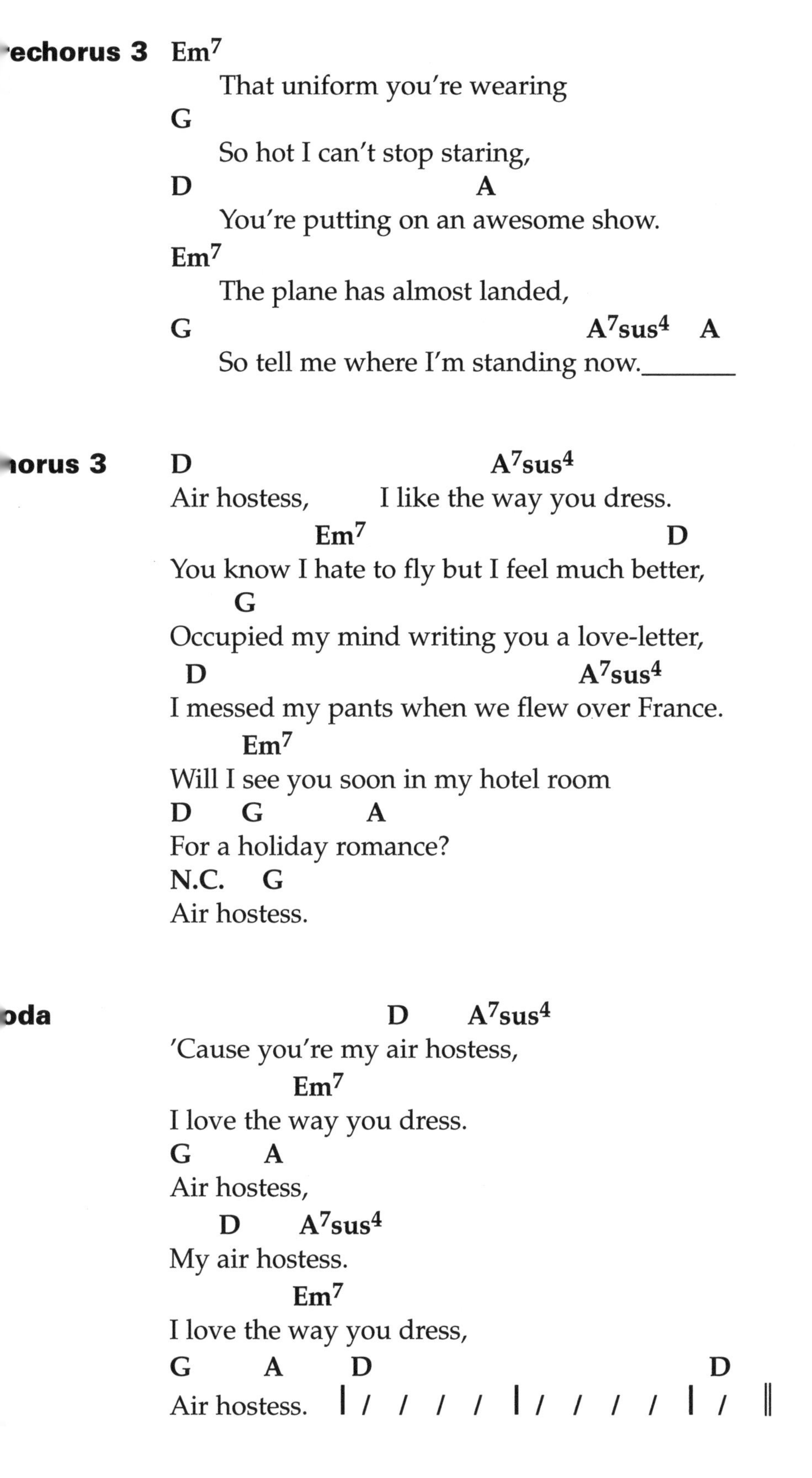

```
echorus 3   Em7
                 That uniform you're wearing
            G
                 So hot I can't stop staring,
            D                          A
                 You're putting on an awesome show.
            Em7
                 The plane has almost landed,
            G                                         A7sus4   A
                 So tell me where I'm standing now._______

horus 3     D                            A7sus4
            Air hostess,       I like the way you dress.
                         Em7                              D
            You know I hate to fly but I feel much better,
                  G
            Occupied my mind writing you a love-letter,
             D                                      A7sus4
            I messed my pants when we flew over France.
                  Em7
            Will I see you soon in my hotel room
            D     G        A
            For a holiday romance?
            N.C.   G
            Air hostess.

oda                            D       A7sus4
            'Cause you're my air hostess,
                       Em7
            I love the way you dress.
            G      A
            Air hostess,
                D      A7sus4
            My air hostess.
                       Em7
            I love the way you dress,
            G      A      D                             D
            Air hostess.  | /  /  /  /  | /  /  /  /  | /  ||
```

# *BRITNEY*

*Words and Music by*
*JAMES BOURNE, JOHN McLAUGHLIN AND STEVE ROBSON*

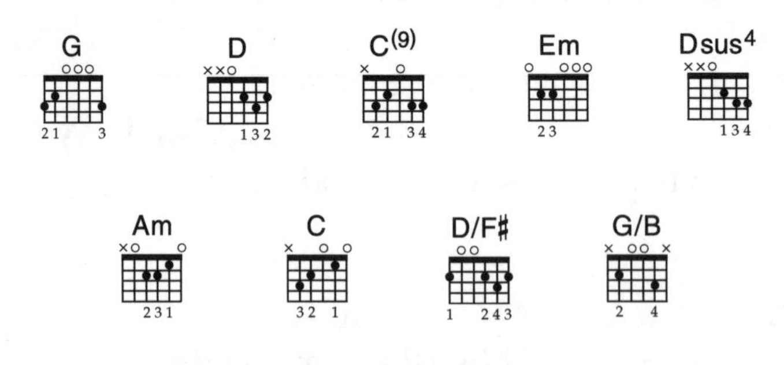


**Capo 2nd fret**

♩ = 170

**Intro**

```
    G    D       C(9)          G    D
4/4 | /  /  /  / | /  /  /  /  | /  /  /  /  ||
```

**Verse 1**

```
C(9)                 G
      Your face is everywhere I go now
                        Em
And you're on every television show now.
C            D          Dsus4
Baby,   I     need you.
                    G
You're everything I want in someone,
                    Em
But you don't even know who I am,
C          D               Dsus4
Baby, why should you?
```

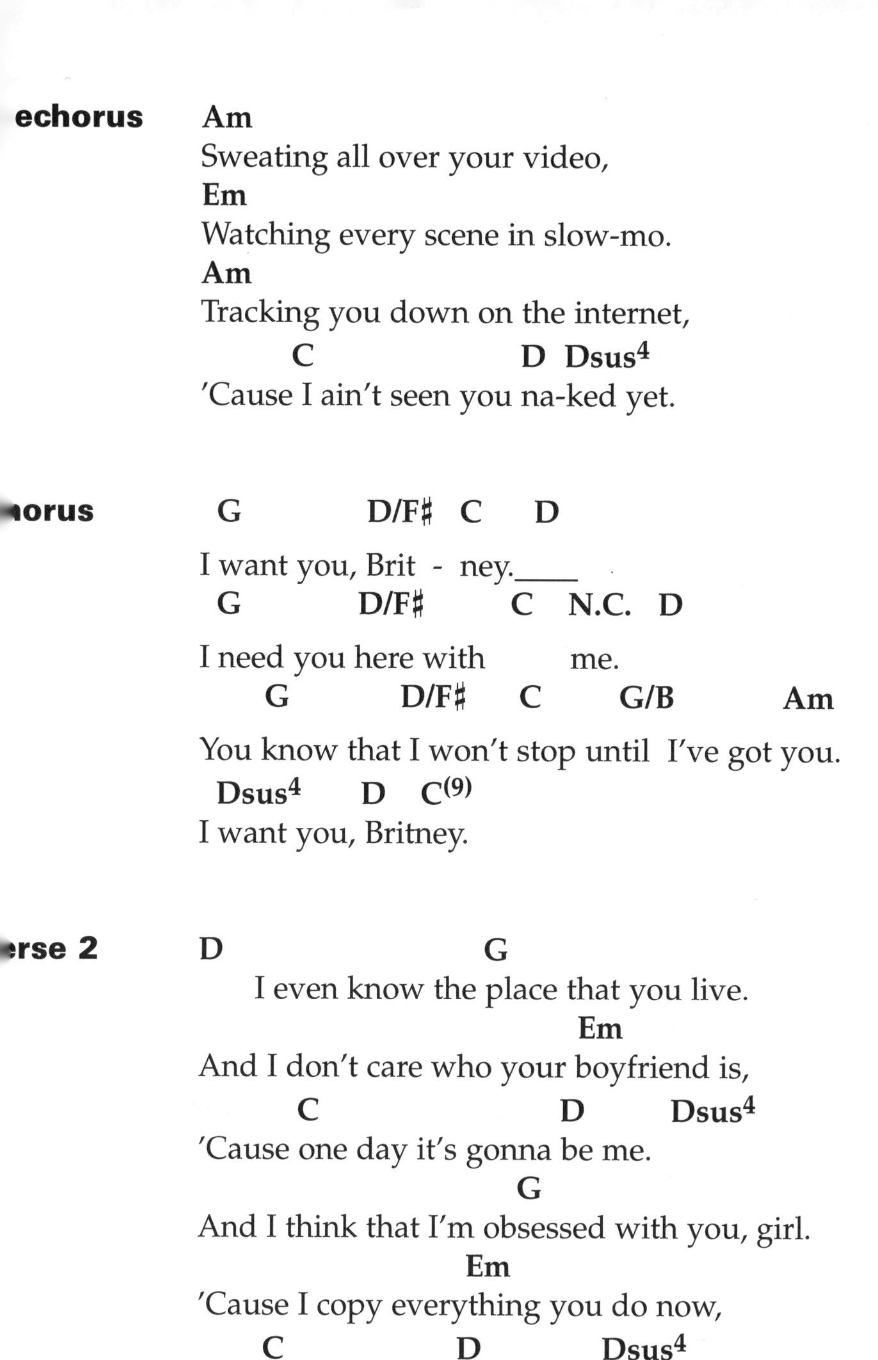

**echorus**

**Am**
Sweating all over your video,
**Em**
Watching every scene in slow-mo.
**Am**
Tracking you down on the internet,
**C** **D** **Dsus4**
'Cause I ain't seen you na-ked yet.

**orus**

**G** **D/F♯** **C** **D**
I want you, Brit - ney.____
**G** **D/F♯** **C** **N.C.** **D**
I need you here with me.
**G** **D/F♯** **C** **G/B** **Am**
You know that I won't stop until I've got you.
**Dsus4** **D** **C(9)**
I want you, Britney.

**erse 2**

**D** **G**
I even know the place that you live.
**Em**
And I don't care who your boyfriend is,
**C** **D** **Dsus4**
'Cause one day it's gonna be me.
**G**
And I think that I'm obsessed with you, girl.
**Em**
'Cause I copy everything you do now,
**C** **D** **Dsus4**
And Pepsi lets me taste you.

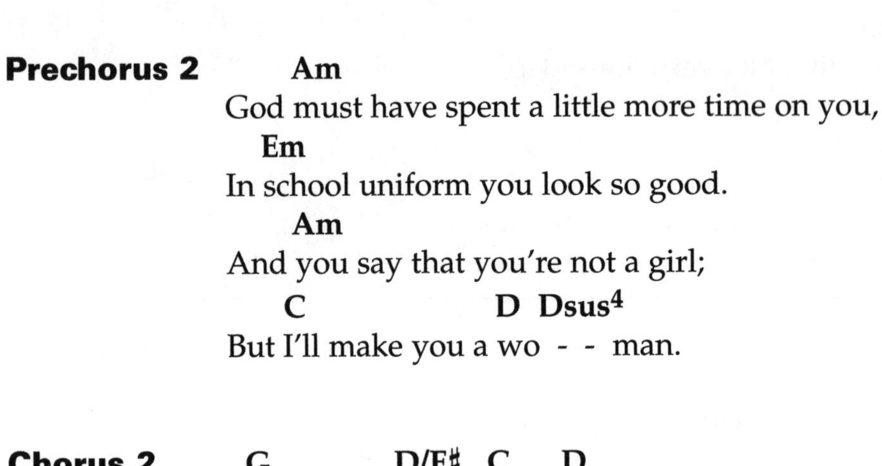

**Prechorus 2**

Am
God must have spent a little more time on you,
Em
In school uniform you look so good.
Am
And you say that you're not a girl;
C D Dsus4
But I'll make you a wo - - man.

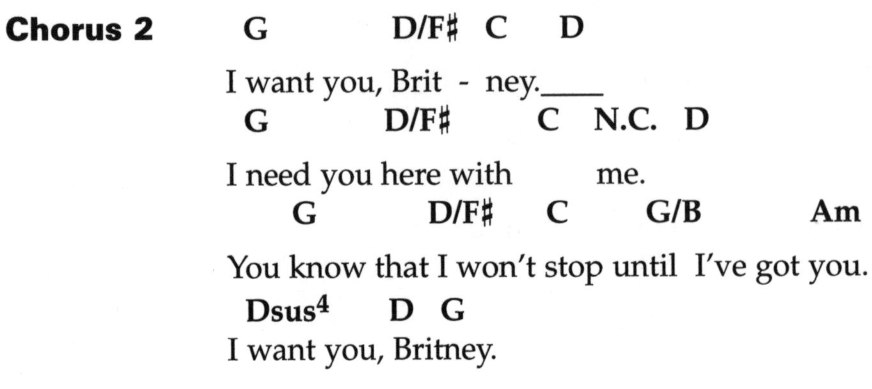

**Chorus 2**

G D/F♯ C D
I want you, Brit - ney.____
G D/F♯ C N.C. D
I need you here with me.
G D/F♯ C G/B Am
You know that I won't stop until I've got you.
Dsus4 D G
I want you, Britney.

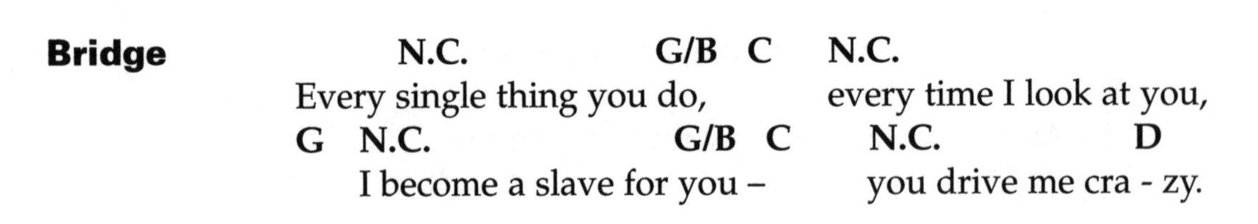

**Bridge**

N.C. G/B C N.C.
Every single thing you do, every time I look at you,
G N.C. G/B C N.C. D
I become a slave for you – you drive me cra - zy.

**Chorus 3**

G D/F♯ C G/B Am
You know that I won't stop until I've got you.
Dsus4 D G
I want you, Britney.

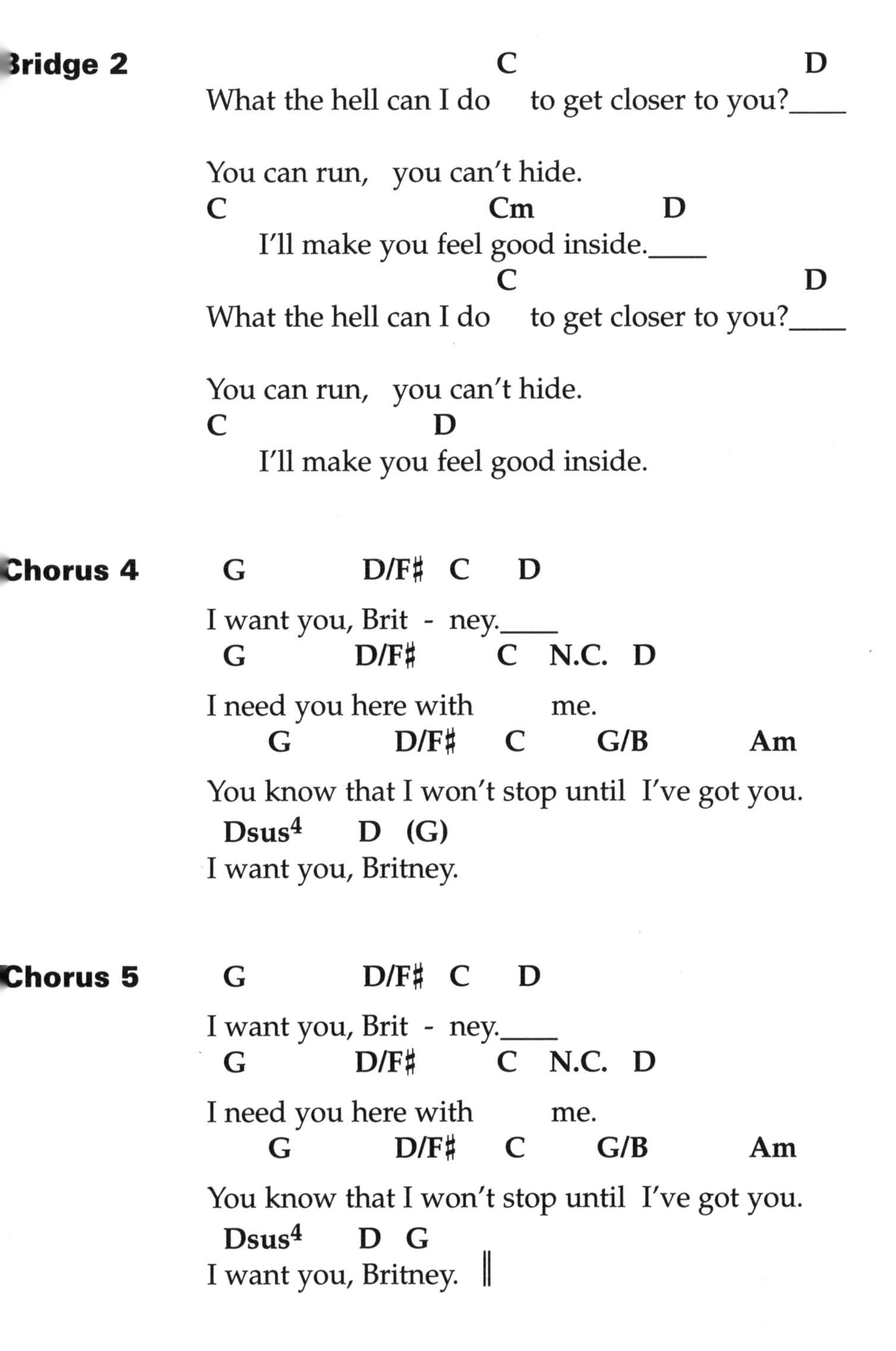

**Bridge 2**

```
                              C                   D
What the hell can I do    to get closer to you?____

You can run,   you can't hide.
C                        Cm          D
     I'll make you feel good inside.____
                              C                   D
What the hell can I do    to get closer to you?____

You can run,   you can't hide.
C                    D
     I'll make you feel good inside.
```

**Chorus 4**

```
  G          D/F♯  C    D
I want you, Brit  -  ney.____
  G          D/F♯       C   N.C.  D
I need you here with        me.
      G          D/F♯    C      G/B        Am
You know that I won't stop until  I've got you.
  Dsus⁴      D   (G)
I want you, Britney.
```

**Chorus 5**

```
  G          D/F♯  C    D
I want you, Brit  -  ney.____
  G          D/F♯       C   N.C.  D
I need you here with        me.
      G          D/F♯    C      G/B        Am
You know that I won't stop until  I've got you.
  Dsus⁴      D   G
I want you, Britney.  ‖
```

# CRASHED THE WEDDING

*Words and Music by*
*JAMES BOURNE AND TOM FLETCHER*

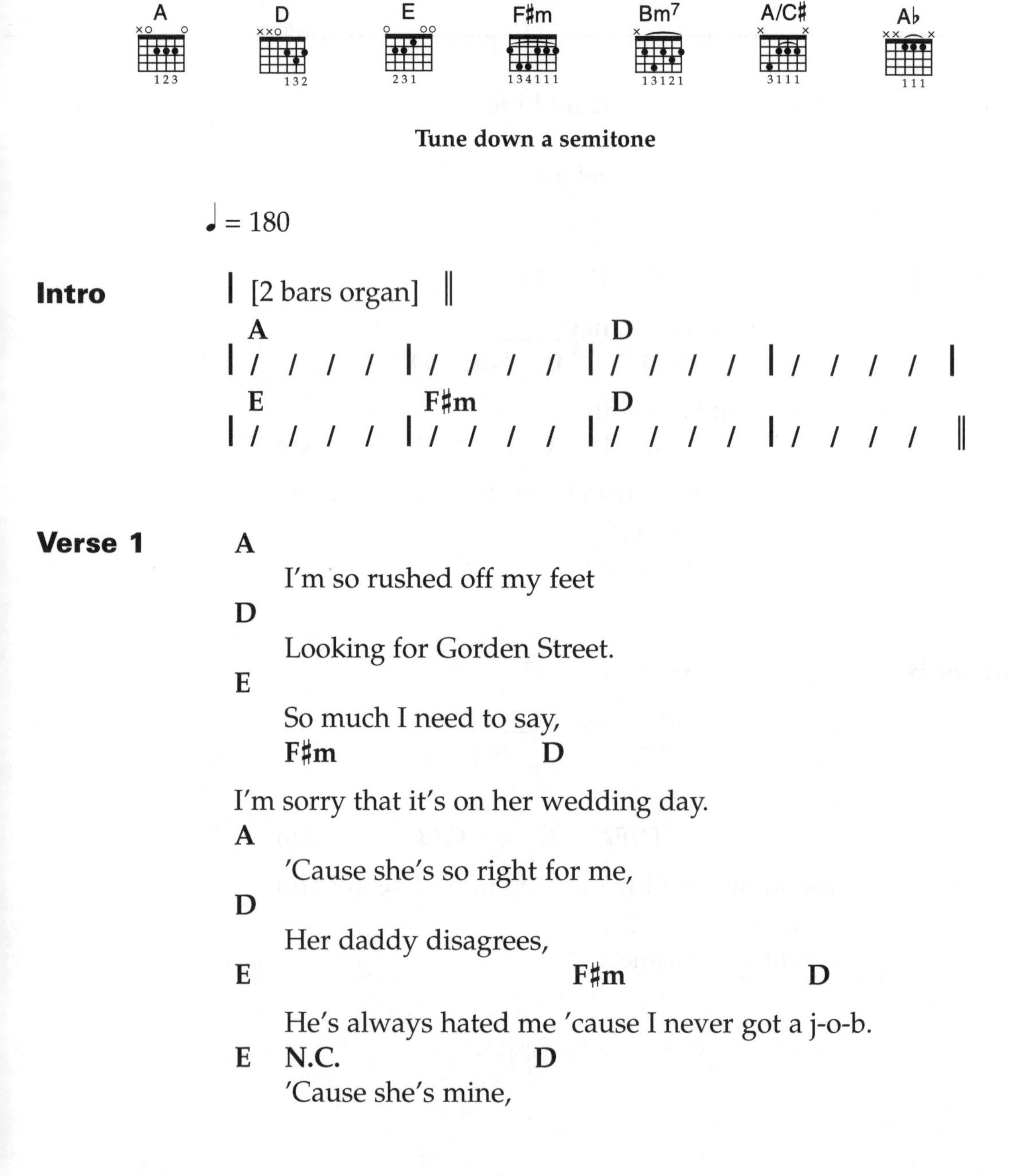


**Tune down a semitone**

♩ = 180

**Intro** | [2 bars organ] ‖

```
 A                      D
| / / / / | / / / / | / / / / | / / / / |
 E         F♯m          D
| / / / / | / / / / | / / / / | / / / / ‖
```

**Verse 1**

```
A
      I'm so rushed off my feet
D
      Looking for Gorden Street.
E
      So much I need to say,
      F♯m                D
I'm sorry that it's on her wedding day.
A
      'Cause she's so right for me,
D
      Her daddy disagrees,
E                              F♯m               D
      He's always hated me 'cause I never got a j-o-b.
E     N.C.                D
      'Cause she's mine,
```

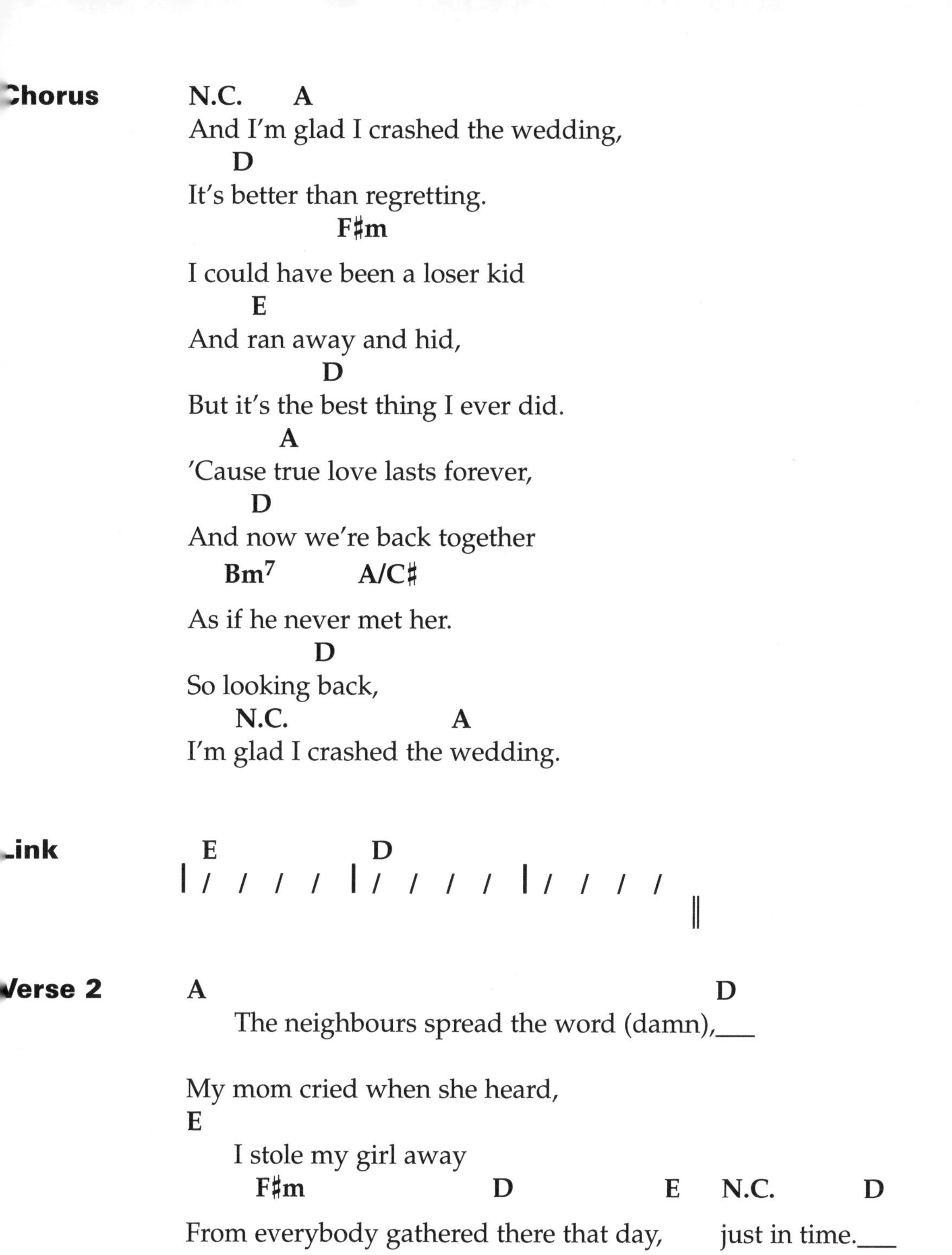

**Chorus**

N.C. A
And I'm glad I crashed the wedding,
D
It's better than regretting.
F♯m
I could have been a loser kid
E
And ran away and hid,
D
But it's the best thing I ever did.
A
'Cause true love lasts forever,
D
And now we're back together
Bm7 A/C♯
As if he never met her.
D
So looking back,
N.C. A
I'm glad I crashed the wedding.

**Link**

E D
| / / / / | / / / / | / / / / ‖

**Verse 2**

A D
The neighbours spread the word (damn),___
My mom cried when she heard,
E
I stole my girl away
F♯m D E N.C. D
From everybody gathered there that day, just in time.___

**Chorus 2**

```
N.C.      A
And I'm glad I crashed the wedding,
     D
It's better than regretting.
                F♯m
I could have been a loser kid
       E
And ran away and hid,
               D
But it's the best thing I ever did.
          A
'Cause true love lasts forever,
       D
And now we're back together
    Bm7          A/C♯
As if he never met her.
              D
So looking back,
    N.C.                A
I'm glad I crashed the wedding.
```

**Bridge**

```
A                          Bm7  A/C♯                          D
     Don't waste time being mad at me for taking her away,
                                          Bm7
'Cause anyway she didn't want to stay.
A/C♯                                      D
     So please believe me when I say
```

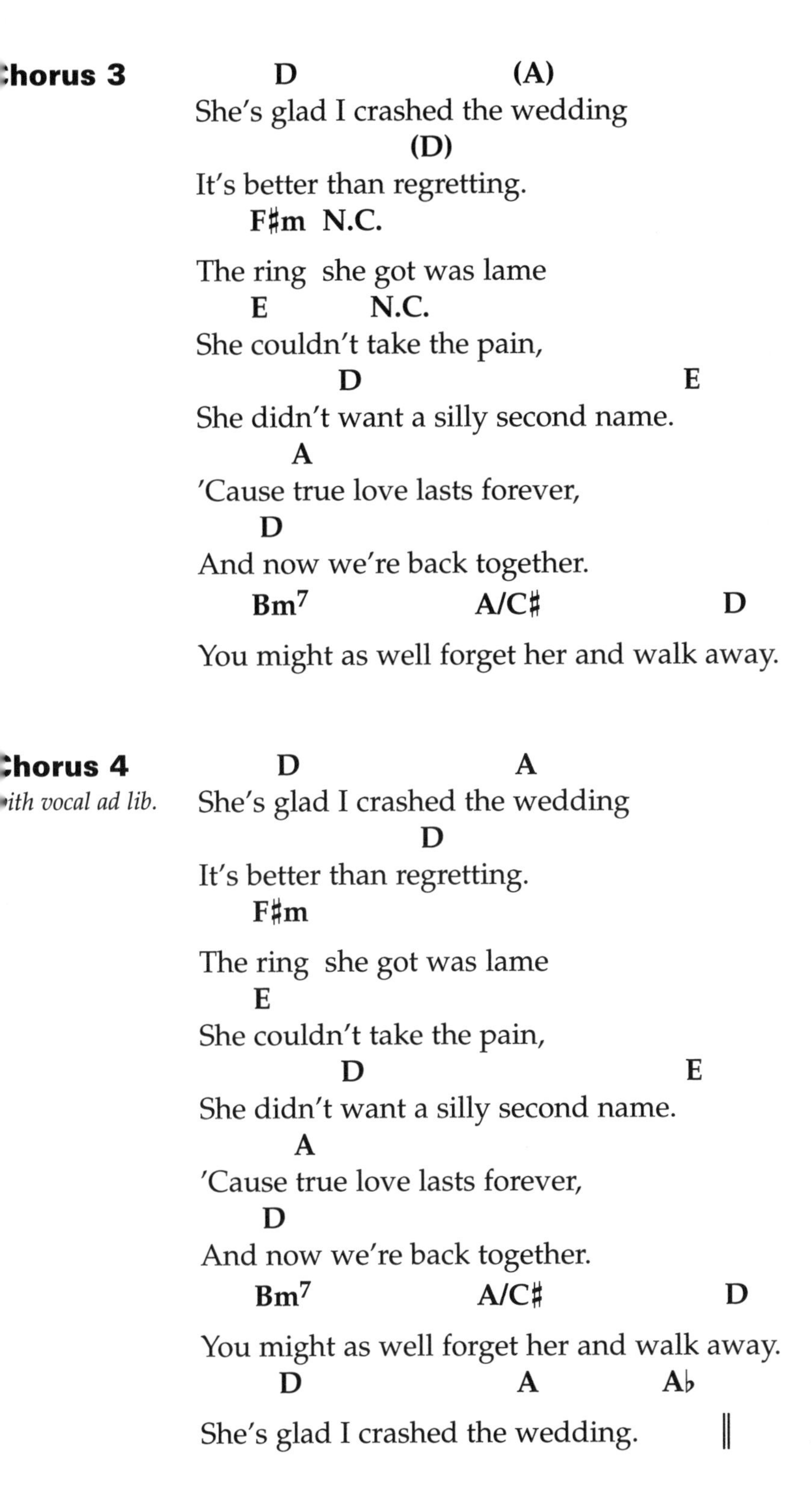
Chorus 3
D (A)
She's glad I crashed the wedding
(D)
It's better than regretting.
F♯m N.C.
The ring she got was lame
E N.C.
She couldn't take the pain,
D E
She didn't want a silly second name.
A
'Cause true love lasts forever,
D
And now we're back together.
Bm7 A/C♯ D
You might as well forget her and walk away.
Chorus 4
with vocal ad lib.
D A
She's glad I crashed the wedding
D
It's better than regretting.
F♯m
The ring she got was lame
E
She couldn't take the pain,
D E
She didn't want a silly second name.
A
'Cause true love lasts forever,
D
And now we're back together.
Bm7 A/C♯ D
You might as well forget her and walk away.
D A A♭
She's glad I crashed the wedding. ‖

# DAWSON'S GEEK

*Words and Music by*
*JAMES BOURNE, MATHEW SARGEANT,*
*AND CHARLIE SIMPSON*

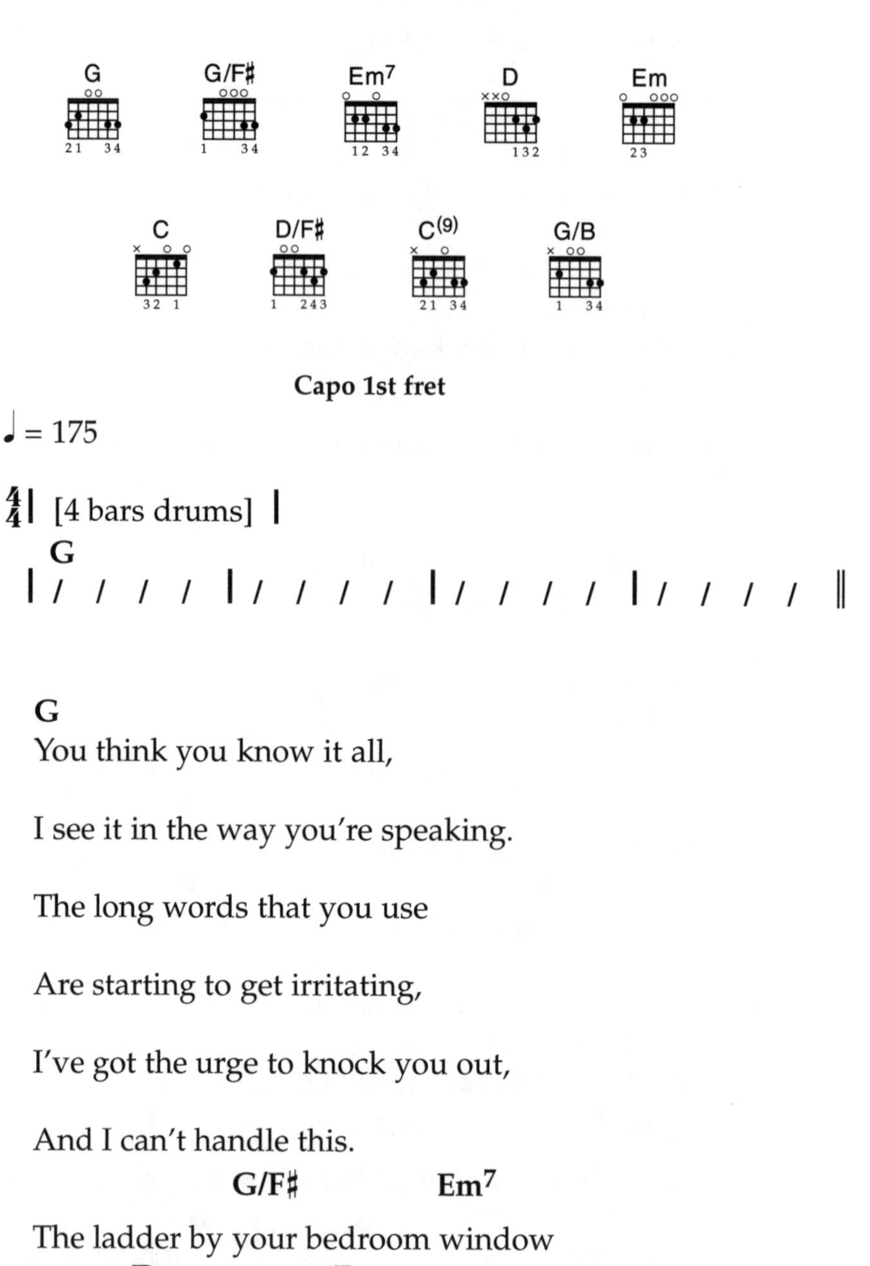


**Capo 1st fret**

♩ = 175

**Intro** 4/4 | [4 bars drums] |

**G**
| / / / / | / / / / | / / / / | / / / / ||

**Verse 1**

**G**
You think you know it all,

I see it in the way you're speaking.

The long words that you use

Are starting to get irritating,

I've got the urge to knock you out,

And I can't handle this.

**G/F♯** **Em7**
The ladder by your bedroom window

**D** **Em**
Really takes the piss.

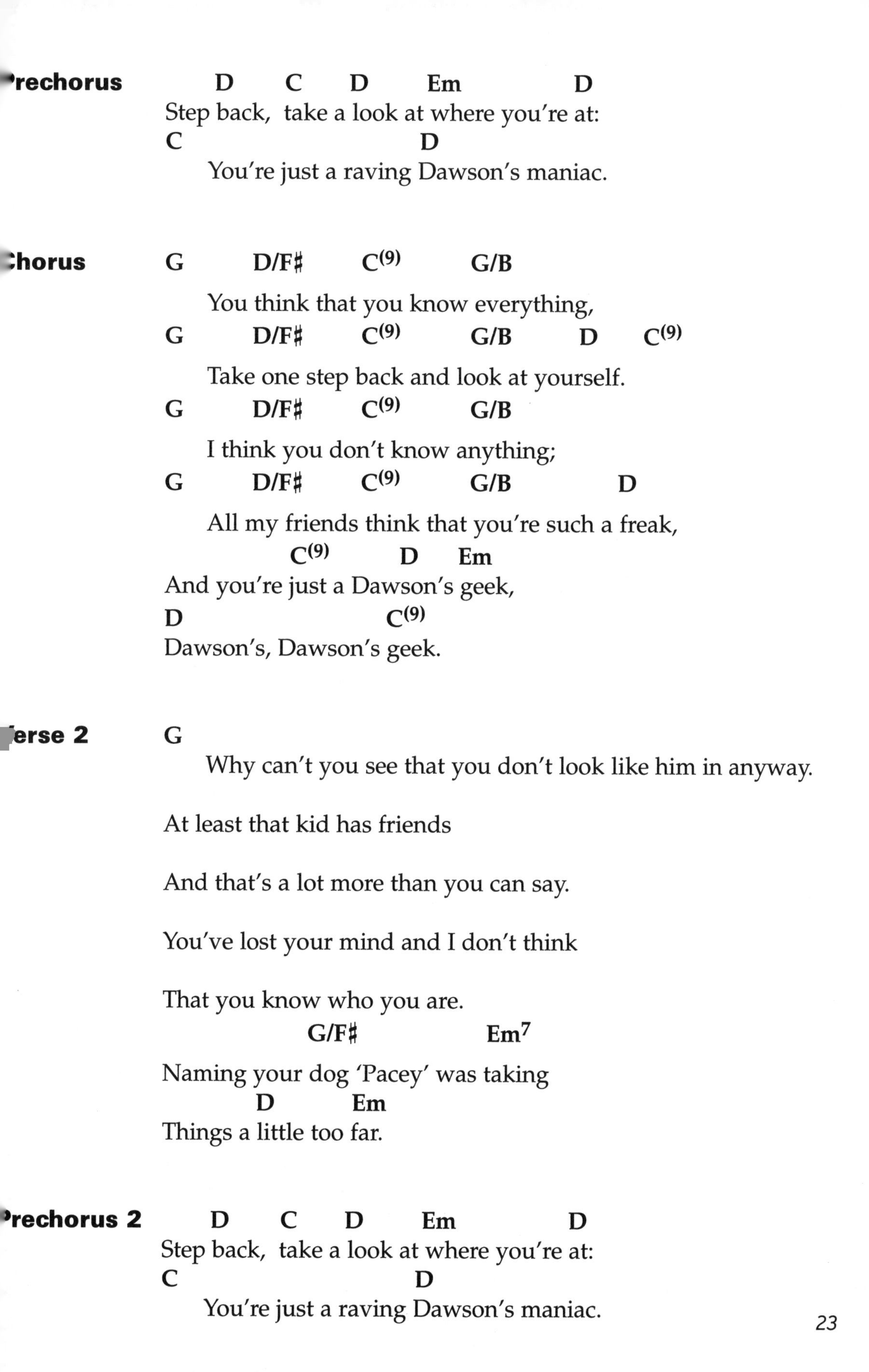

**Prechorus**

D C D Em D
Step back, take a look at where you're at:
C D
You're just a raving Dawson's maniac.

**Chorus**

G D/F♯ $C^{(9)}$ G/B
You think that you know everything,
G D/F♯ $C^{(9)}$ G/B D $C^{(9)}$
Take one step back and look at yourself.
G D/F♯ $C^{(9)}$ G/B
I think you don't know anything;
G D/F♯ $C^{(9)}$ G/B D
All my friends think that you're such a freak,
$C^{(9)}$ D Em
And you're just a Dawson's geek,
D $C^{(9)}$
Dawson's, Dawson's geek.

**Verse 2**

G
Why can't you see that you don't look like him in anyway.

At least that kid has friends

And that's a lot more than you can say.

You've lost your mind and I don't think

That you know who you are.
G/F♯ $Em^7$
Naming your dog 'Pacey' was taking
D Em
Things a little too far.

**Prechorus 2**

D C D Em D
Step back, take a look at where you're at:
C D
You're just a raving Dawson's maniac.

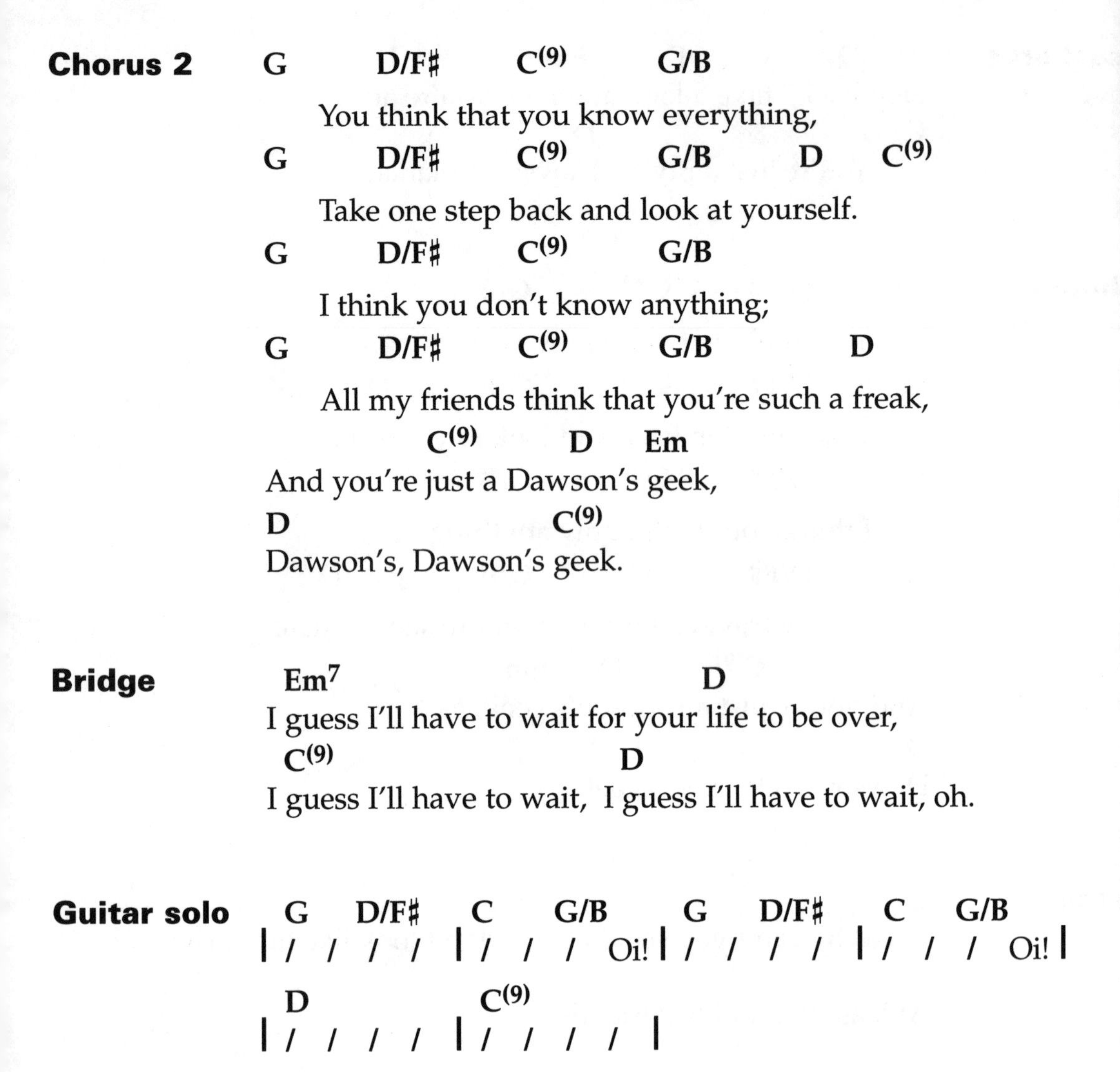

**Chorus 2**

G D/F♯ C(9) G/B
You think that you know everything,
G D/F♯ C(9) G/B D C(9)
Take one step back and look at yourself.
G D/F♯ C(9) G/B
I think you don't know anything;
G D/F♯ C(9) G/B D
All my friends think that you're such a freak,
C(9) D Em
And you're just a Dawson's geek,
D C(9)
Dawson's, Dawson's geek.

**Bridge**

Em7 D
I guess I'll have to wait for your life to be over,
C(9) D
I guess I'll have to wait, I guess I'll have to wait, oh.

**Guitar solo**

G D/F♯ C G/B G D/F♯ C G/B
| / / / / | / / / Oi! | / / / / | / / / Oi! |
D C(9)
| / / / / | / / / / |

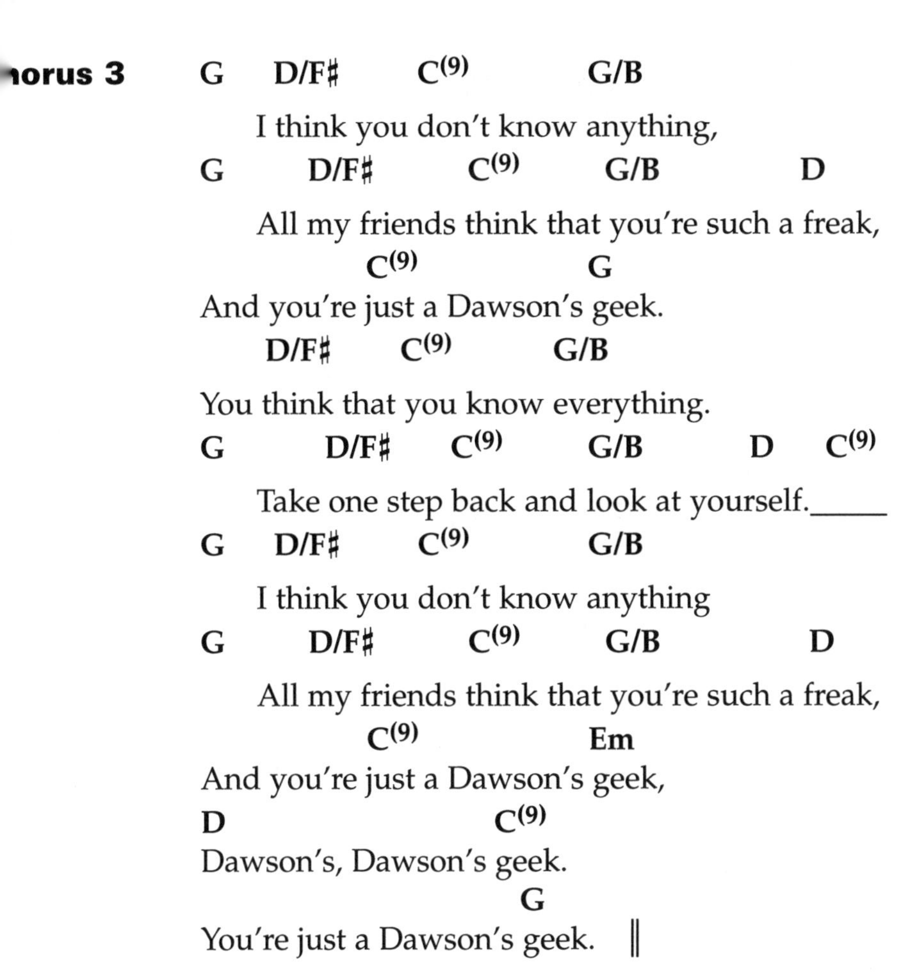

**horus 3**

```
G    D/F♯       C(9)          G/B
     I think you don't know anything,
G       D/F♯        C(9)      G/B          D
     All my friends think that you're such a freak,
              C(9)              G
And you're just a Dawson's geek.
     D/F♯      C(9)         G/B
You think that you know everything.
G         D/F♯     C(9)         G/B         D    C(9)
     Take one step back and look at yourself.______
G    D/F♯       C(9)          G/B
     I think you don't know anything
G       D/F♯        C(9)      G/B           D
     All my friends think that you're such a freak,
              C(9)              Em
And you're just a Dawson's geek,
D                       C(9)
Dawson's, Dawson's geek.
                          G
You're just a Dawson's geek.   ‖
```

# *LOSER KID*

*Words and Music by*
*JAMES BOURNE, MATHEW SARGEANT,*
*AND CHARLIE SIMPSON*

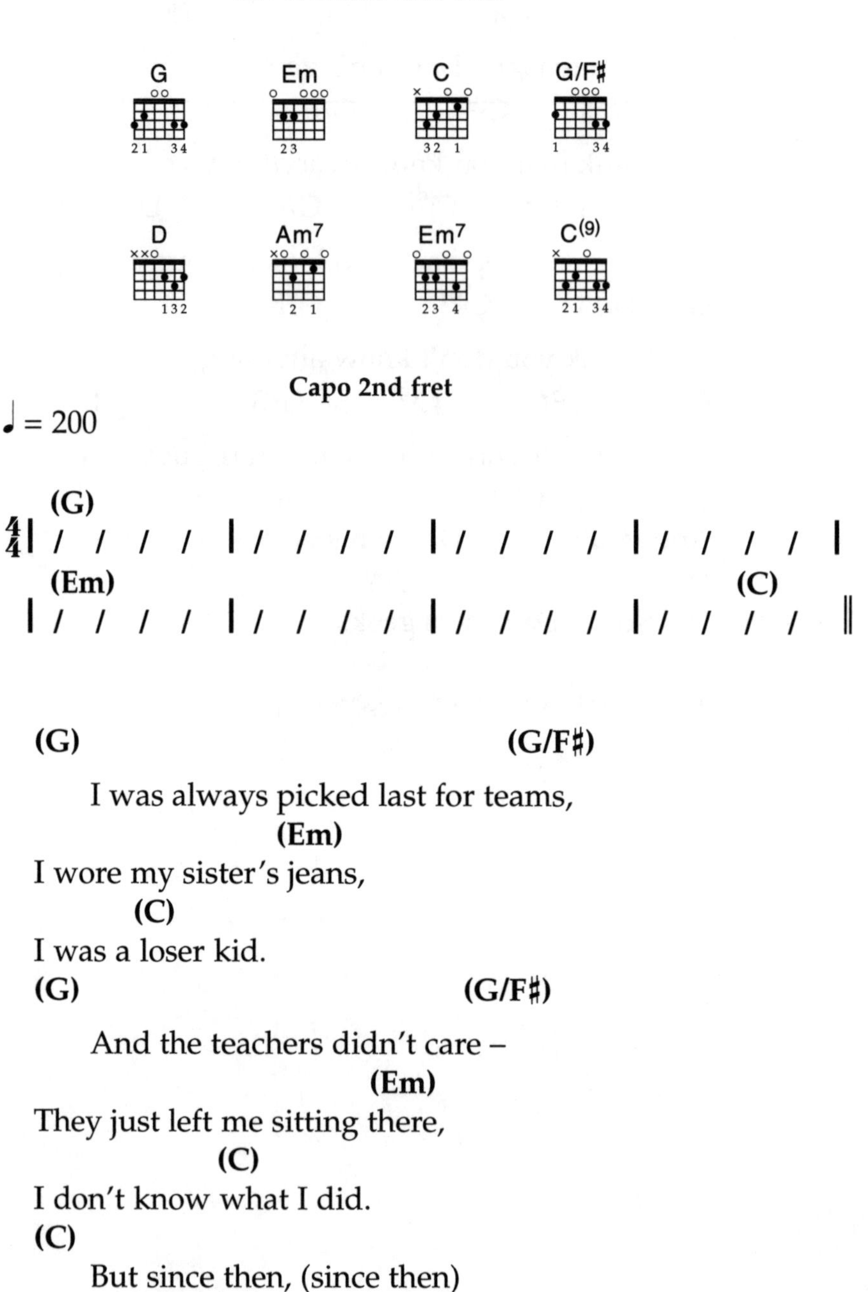


**Capo 2nd fret**

♩ = 200

**Intro**

(G)
4/4 | / / / / | / / / / | / / / / | / / / / |
(Em)                                    (C)
| / / / / | / / / / | / / / / | / / / / ||

**Verse 1**

**(G)** **(G/F♯)**
I was always picked last for teams,
**(Em)**
I wore my sister's jeans,
**(C)**
I was a loser kid.
**(G)** **(G/F♯)**
And the teachers didn't care –
**(Em)**
They just left me sitting there,
**(C)**
I don't know what I did.
**(C)**
But since then, (since then)
**Em** **D**
How the tides have turned.____

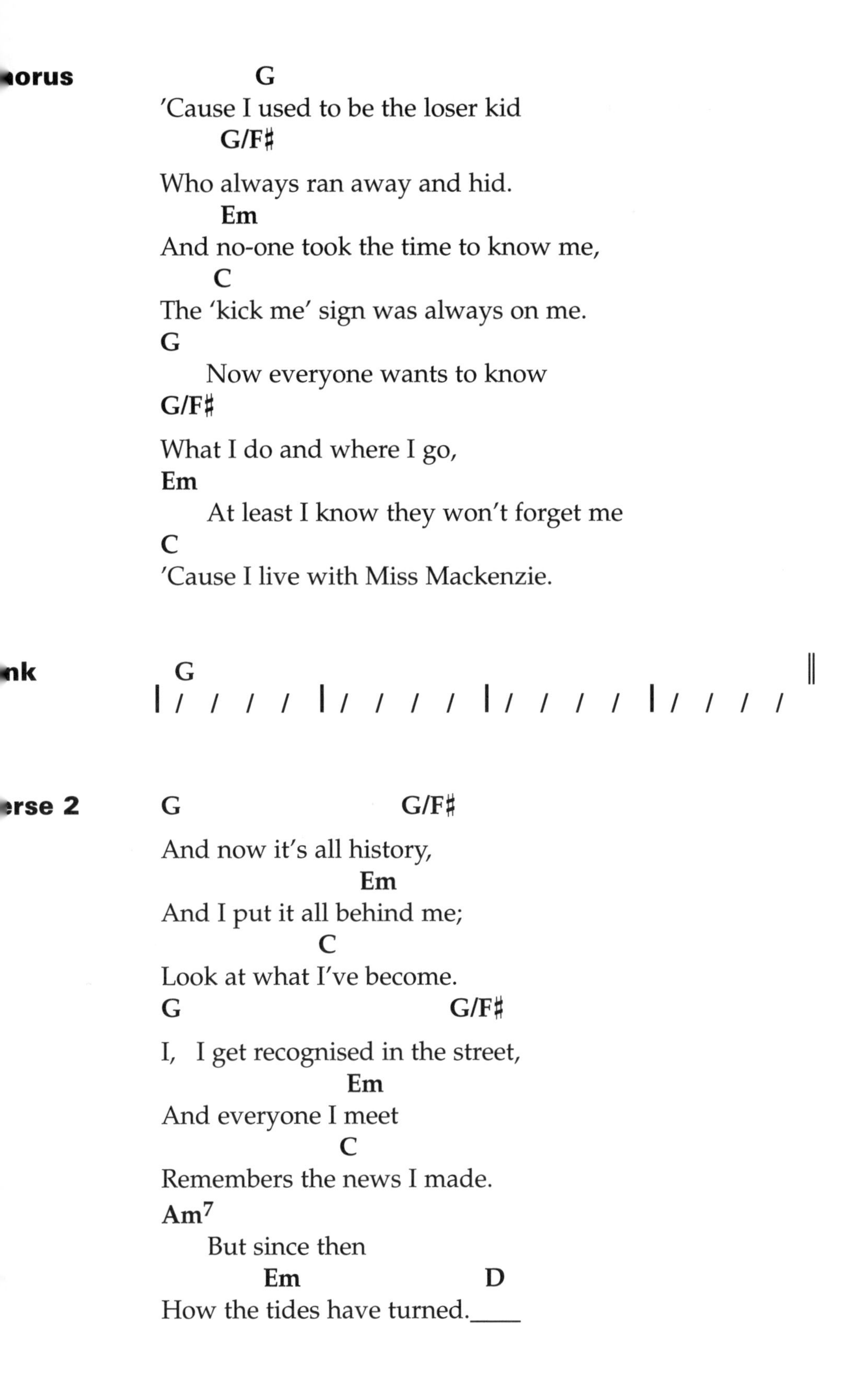
orus
G
'Cause I used to be the loser kid
G/F♯
Who always ran away and hid.
Em
And no-one took the time to know me,
C
The 'kick me' sign was always on me.
G
Now everyone wants to know
G/F♯
What I do and where I go,
Em
At least I know they won't forget me
C
'Cause I live with Miss Mackenzie.
nk
G
| / / / / | / / / / | / / / / | / / / / ||
rse 2
G G/F♯
And now it's all history,
Em
And I put it all behind me;
C
Look at what I've become.
G G/F♯
I, I get recognised in the street,
Em
And everyone I meet
C
Remembers the news I made.
Am7
But since then
Em D
How the tides have turned.____

**Chorus 2**

G
'Cause I used to be the loser kid
G/F♯
Who always ran away and hid.
Em
And no-one took the time to know me,
C
The 'kick me' sign was always on me.
G
Now everyone wants to know
G/F♯
What I do and where I go,
Em
At least I know they won't forget me
C
'Cause I live with Miss Mackenzie.

**Bridge**

Em$^7$ D
When I see the way you look at me,
C$^{(9)}$ D
It takes me back to how it used to be.
Em$^7$
And still it's clear,
D
The way you locked the classroom door
C$^{(9)}$
And whispered in my ear,
D Em
"You're what I go to school for,
D C$^{(9)}$ D
You are the one I go to school for."

**Instrumental**

G G/F♯
‖: / / / / | / / / / | / / / / | / / / / |
Em C
| / / / / | / / / / | / / / / | / / / / :‖

**horus 3**

*h vocal ad lib.*

G
'Cause I used to be the loser kid
G/F♯
Who always ran away and hid.
Em
And no-one took the time to know me,
C
The 'kick me' sign was always on me.
G
Now everyone wants to know
G/F♯
What I do and where I go,
Em
At least I know they won't forget me
C
'Cause I live with Miss Mackenzie.

**horus 4**

G
'Cause I used to be the loser kid
G/F♯
Who always ran away and hid.
Em
And no-one took the time to know me,
C
The 'kick me' sign was always on me.
G
Now everyone wants to know
G/F♯
What I do and where I go,
Em
At least I know they won't forget me
C
'Cause I live with Miss Mackenzie.

**oda**

G
𝄆 'Cause I used to be.
G/F♯ Em C
No-one took the time to know me. 𝄇 *repeat to fade*
'Cause I used to be.____

# MEET YOU THERE

*Words and Music by*
CHARLIE SIMPSON AND JAMES BOURNE

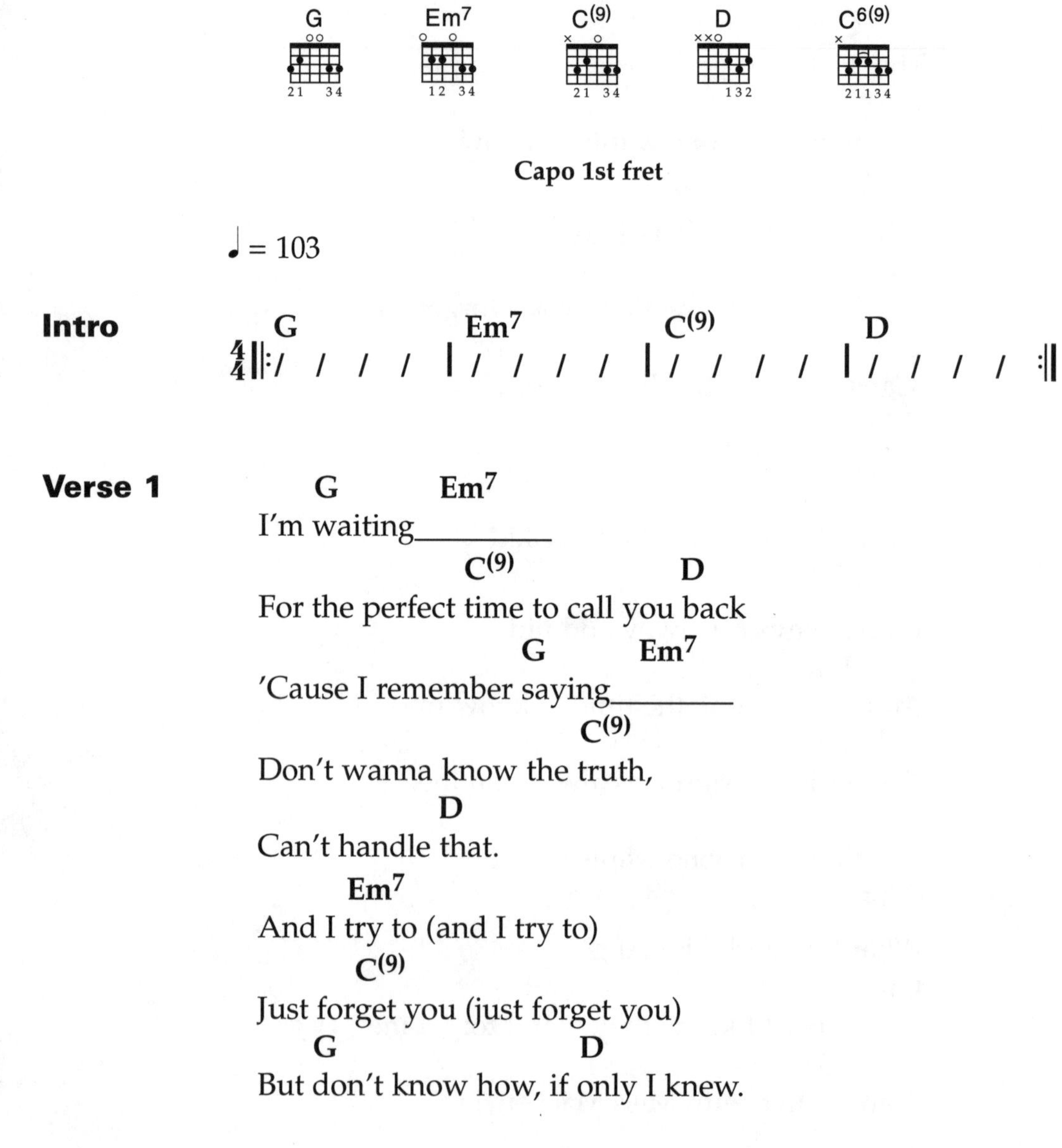


**Capo 1st fret**

♩ = 103

**Intro**

```
   G              Em7            C(9)           D
4/4 ||: /  /  /  / | /  /  /  / | /  /  /  / | /  /  /  / :||
```

**Verse 1**

```
      G          Em7
I'm waiting__________
                    C(9)            D
For the perfect time to call you back
                         G          Em7
'Cause I remember saying__________
                              C(9)
Don't wanna know the truth,
                  D
Can't handle that.
        Em7
And I try to (and I try to)
        C(9)
Just forget you (just forget you)
      G                      D
But don't know how, if only I knew.
```

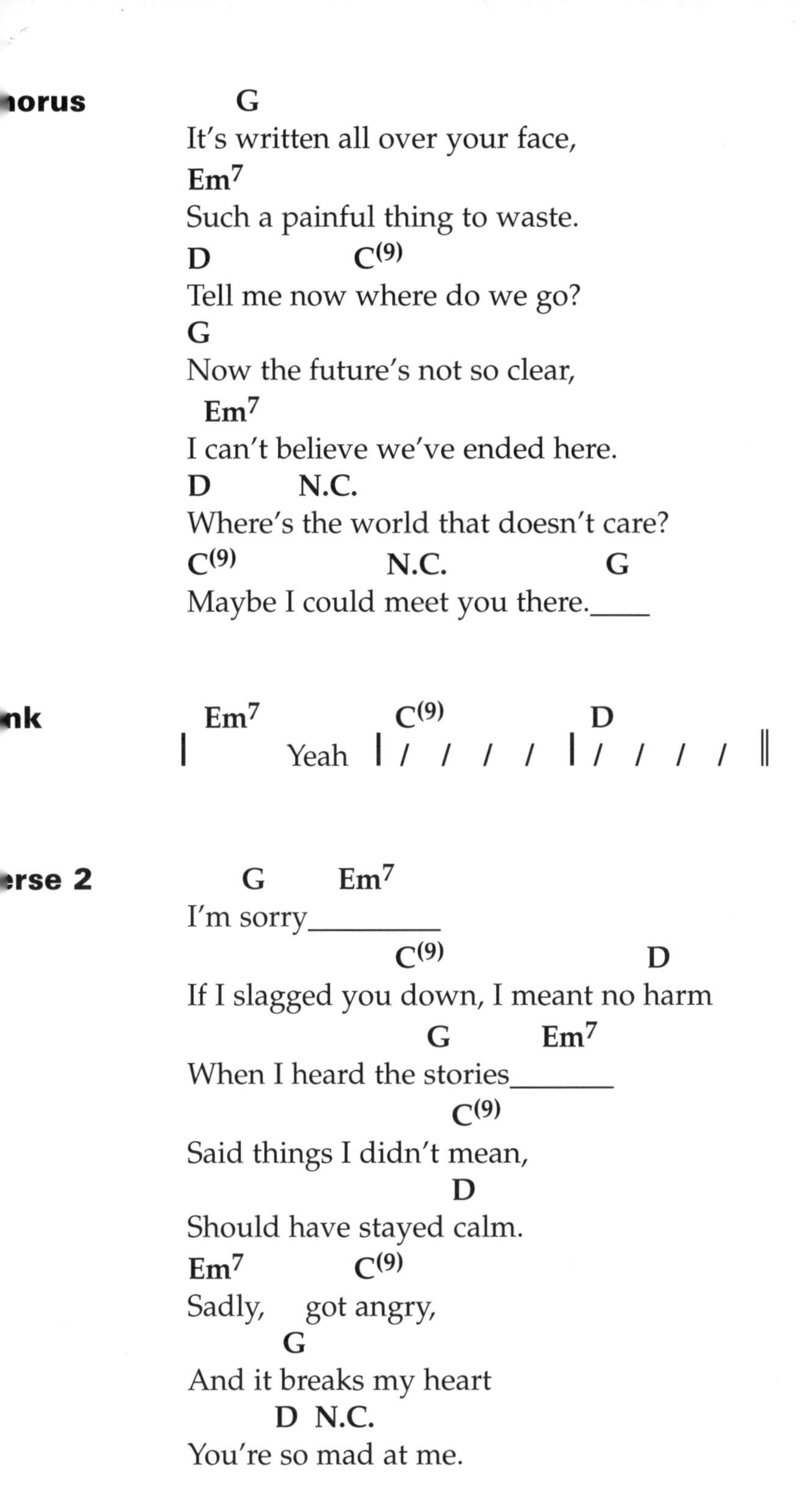

**horus**

**G**
It's written all over your face,
**Em7**
Such a painful thing to waste.
**D C(9)**
Tell me now where do we go?
**G**
Now the future's not so clear,
**Em7**
I can't believe we've ended here.
**D N.C.**
Where's the world that doesn't care?
**C(9) N.C. G**
Maybe I could meet you there.____

**nk**

**Em7 C(9) D**
| Yeah | / / / / | / / / / ||

**rse 2**

**G Em7**
I'm sorry_________
**C(9) D**
If I slagged you down, I meant no harm
**G Em7**
When I heard the stories_______
**C(9)**
Said things I didn't mean,
**D**
Should have stayed calm.
**Em7 C(9)**
Sadly, got angry,
**G**
And it breaks my heart
**D N.C.**
You're so mad at me.

**Chorus 2**

```
   G
It's written all over your face,
Em7
Such a painful thing to waste.
D              C(9)
Tell me now where do we go?
G
Now the future's not so clear,
  Em7
I can't believe we've ended here.
D        N.C.
Where's the world that doesn't care?
C(9)              N.C.            G
Maybe I could meet you there.____
Em7                                C(9)
Maybe I could meet you there.____
D
Maybe I could meet you there.____
```

**Link**

```
  G              Em7              C(9)             D
||: / / / / | / / / / | / / / / | / / / / :||
```

**Chorus 3**

```
   G                              Em7
It's written all over your face, such a painful thing to waste.
D              C(9)
Tell me now where do we go?
G                                  Em7
Now the future's not so clear, I can't believe we've ended here.
D        N.C.
Where's the world that doesn't care?
C(9)              N.C.            C(9)    C6(9)
Maybe I could meet you there._____
C(9)                                      C6(9)
Maybe I could meet you there._____
C(9)
Maybe I should meet you there.  ||
```

# PSYCHO GIRL

*Words and Music by*
JAMES BOURNE AND STEVE ROBSON

**Verse 2**

A C♯/G♯
I can't change her thinking
A C♯/G♯
But she's so good-looking.
Bm7 Dm7
Thinking of her name – it's driving me insane.

**Chorus 2**

A E
She's my psycho girl, my psycho girlfriend.
Bm7 Dm7
Everything I say, she takes it the wrong way.
A E
She's my psycho girl, my living nightmare,
Bm7 Dm7
She's everything I need but I can't stand her.

**Bridge**

A E
We spent the night in, we started fighting.
Bm7 F♯m E
Since then it's never been the same.
Bm7 Dm7
Thinking of her name is driving me insane.

**Chorus 3**

A E
She's my psycho girl, my psycho girlfriend.
Bm7 Dm7
Everything I say, she takes it the wrong way.
A Amaj7
She's my psycho girl, my living nightmare,
Bm7 Dm7
She's everything I need but I can't stand her.

**horus 4**

```
              A                  E
She's my psycho girl,  my psycho girlfriend.
Bm7                         Dm7
Everything I say,   she takes it the wrong way.
              A                  E
She's my psycho girl,  my living nightmare,
      Bm7                        Dm7
She's everything I need but I can't stand her.
```

**horus 5**

```
              A                  E
She's my psycho girl,  my psycho girlfriend.
Bm7                         Dm7
Everything I say,   she takes it the wrong way.
              A                  E
She's my psycho girl,  my living nightmare,
      Bm7                        Dm7
She's everything I need but I can't stand her.
```

**oda**

```
  A          Asus4    A
||: /   /   /          /        :||  repeat to fade
```

# *SLEEPING WITH THE LIGHT ON*

*Words and Music by*
*JAMES BOURNE AND MATHEW SARGEANT*

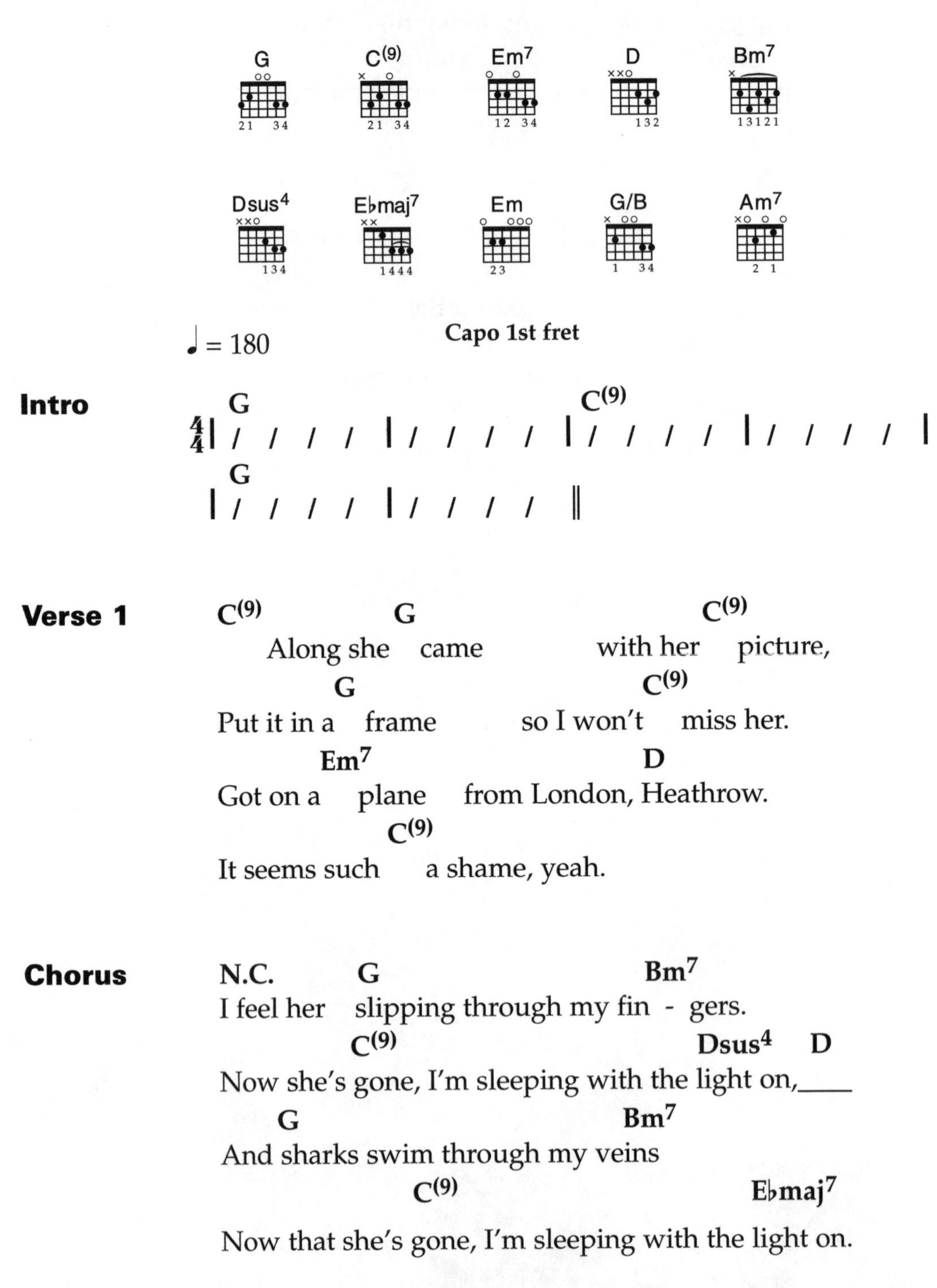

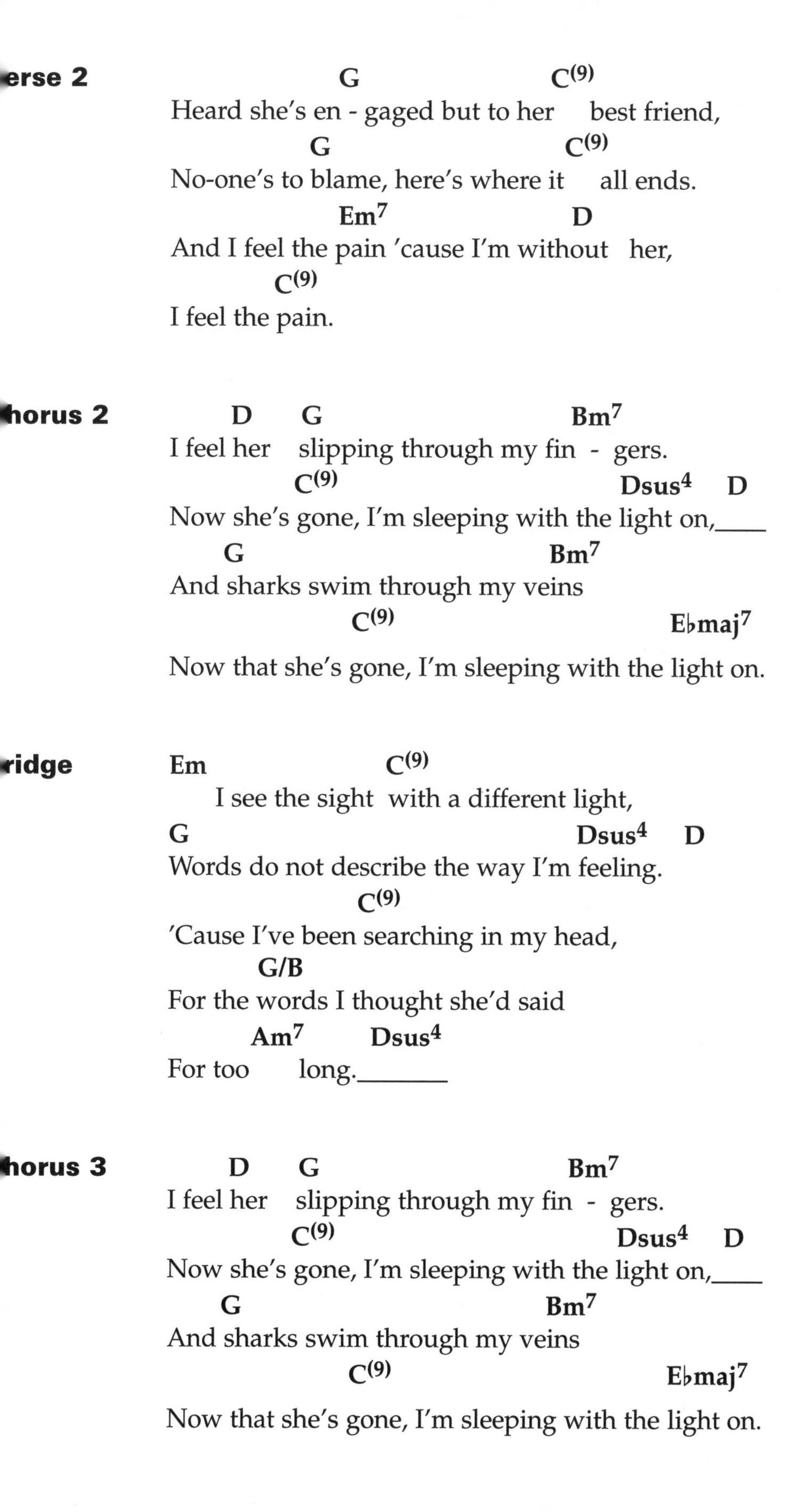

**erse 2**

G C(9)
Heard she's en - gaged but to her best friend,
G C(9)
No-one's to blame, here's where it all ends.
Em7 D
And I feel the pain 'cause I'm without her,
C(9)
I feel the pain.

**horus 2**

D G Bm7
I feel her slipping through my fin - gers.
C(9) Dsus4 D
Now she's gone, I'm sleeping with the light on,____
G Bm7
And sharks swim through my veins
C(9) E♭maj7
Now that she's gone, I'm sleeping with the light on.

**ridge**

Em C(9)
I see the sight with a different light,
G Dsus4 D
Words do not describe the way I'm feeling.
C(9)
'Cause I've been searching in my head,
G/B
For the words I thought she'd said
Am7 Dsus4
For too long.________

**horus 3**

D G Bm7
I feel her slipping through my fin - gers.
C(9) Dsus4 D
Now she's gone, I'm sleeping with the light on,____
G Bm7
And sharks swim through my veins
C(9) E♭maj7
Now that she's gone, I'm sleeping with the light on.

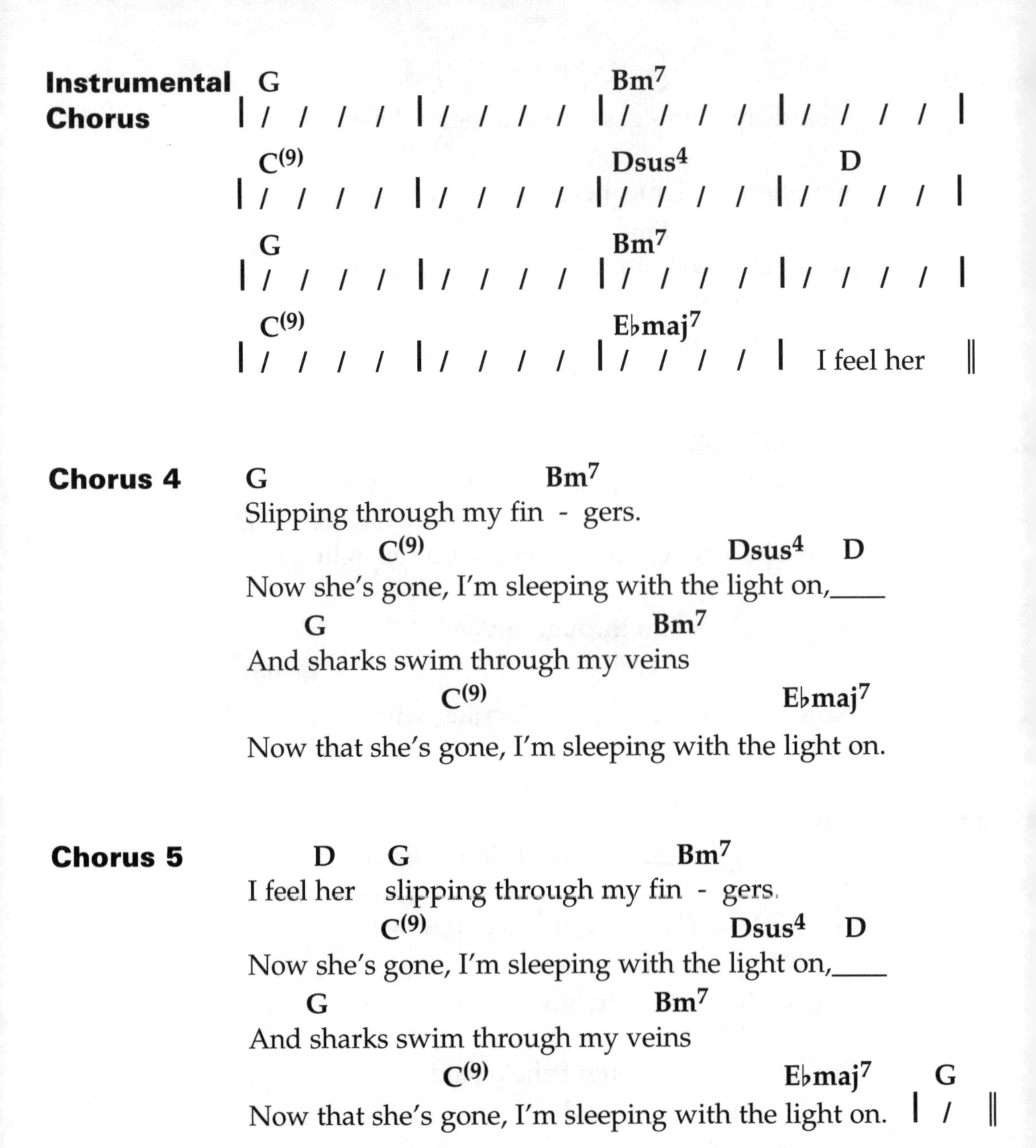
Instrumental Chorus
G Bm7
C(9) Dsus4 D
G Bm7
C(9) E♭maj7
I feel her
Chorus 4
G Bm7
Slipping through my fin - gers.
C(9) Dsus4 D
Now she's gone, I'm sleeping with the light on,
G Bm7
And sharks swim through my veins
C(9) E♭maj7
Now that she's gone, I'm sleeping with the light on.
Chorus 5
D G Bm7
I feel her slipping through my fin - gers.
C(9) Dsus4 D
Now she's gone, I'm sleeping with the light on,
G Bm7
And sharks swim through my veins
C(9) E♭maj7 G
Now that she's gone, I'm sleeping with the light on.

# *THUNDERBIRDS ARE GO*

*Words and Music by*
*MATHEW SARGEANT, CHARLES SIMPSON, JAMES BOURNE,*
*THOMAS FLETCHER AND BARRY GRAY*

B (7fr, 134211) D♯m (6fr, 13421) G♯m (4fr, 134111) E (231)

Em (23) F♯ (134211) G (3fr, 134211) A (5fr, 134211)

♩ = 100

**Intro**

(B)
| / / / / | / / / / | / / / / | / / / / ||

♩ = 120

B D♯m
| / / / / | / / / / | / / / / | / / / / |

G♯m E Em
| / / / / | / / / / | / / / / | / / / / ||

**Verse 1**

**B** **D♯m**
Spring breaks come around and there's no heroes to be found.
**G♯m** **E** **Em**
There's something major going down on Tracy Island (Island).
**B** **D♯m**
Weapons underground keeping the planet safe and sound,
**G♯m**
If someone evil's coming round
**E** **Em**
They should be frightened (frightened).
**G♯m** **F♯**
'Cause now the boys are back in town,
**E** **G** **A**
No strings to hold them down, down._____

**Chorus 2**

B                    G♯m
Don't be mad,  please stop the hating.
F♯               E        Em
Just be glad that they'll be waiting.
B                   G♯m
Friends we have are ever-changing.
F♯                           E
You know the lid's about to blow
          G       N.C.     B
When the Thunderbirds are go.

**Verse 2**

B                                    D♯m
Kids are learning fast, they know the T-birds kick some ass.
           G♯m                              E        Em
Be sure that there's no coming last if you're on their side (their sic
     B                                    D♯m
They always look so cool when spaceships come out of the pool
             G♯m                        E        Em
You know that you'd just be a fool to be a bad guy (bad guy).
      G♯m                    F♯
'Cause now the boys are back in town
                        E        G      A
No strings to hold them down,   down.____

**Chorus 2**

B                    G♯m
Don't be mad,  please stop the hating.
F♯               E        Em
Just be glad that they'll be waiting.
B                   G♯m
Friends we have are ever-changing.
F♯                           E
You know the lid's about to blow
          G       A      B
When the Thunderbirds are go.

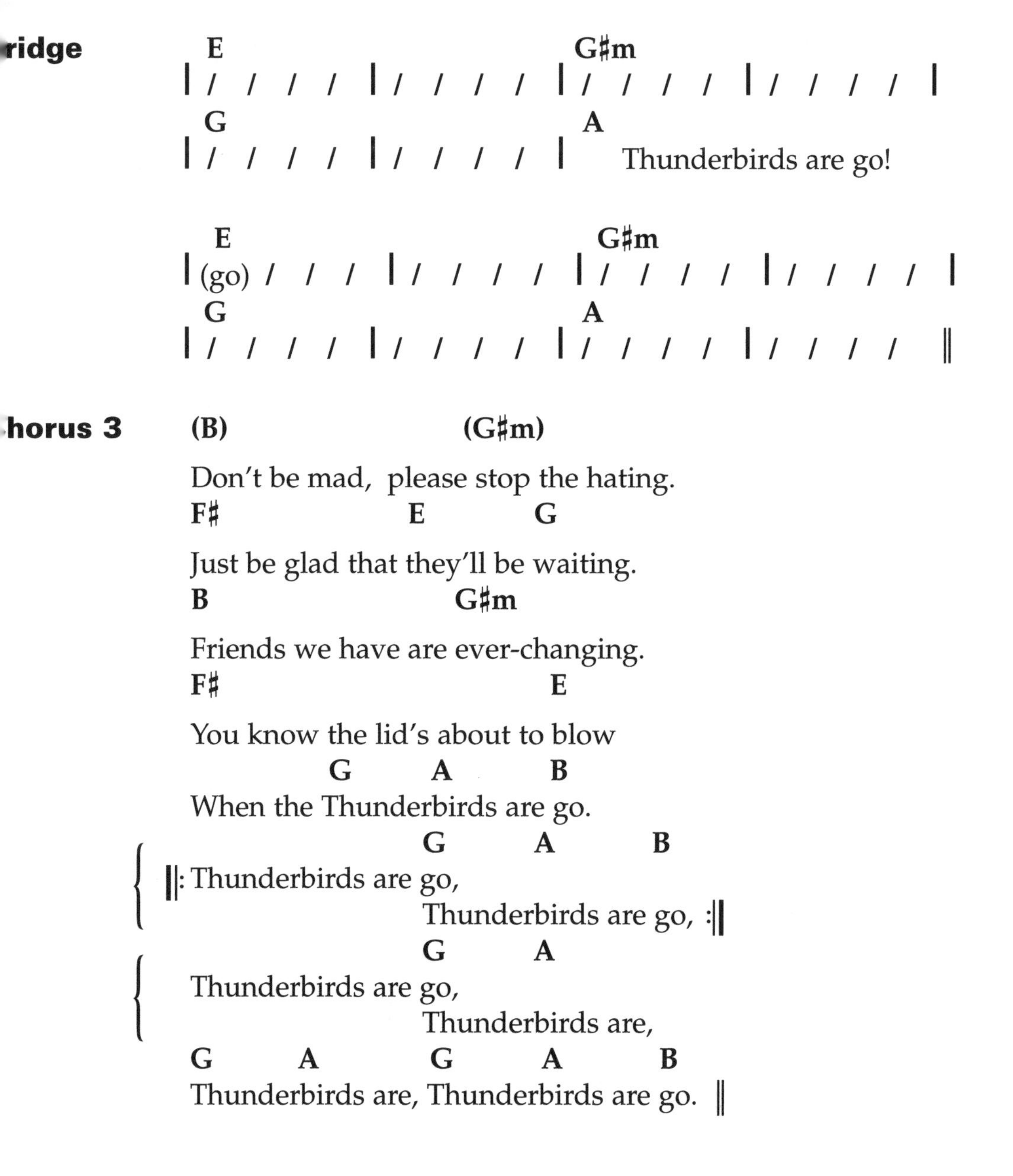

ridge
E
G♯m
G
A
Thunderbirds are go!
E
G♯m
(go)
G
A
horus 3
(B)
(G♯m)
Don't be mad, please stop the hating.
F♯
E
G
Just be glad that they'll be waiting.
B
G♯m
Friends we have are ever-changing.
F♯
E
You know the lid's about to blow
G
A
B
When the Thunderbirds are go.
G
A
B
Thunderbirds are go,
Thunderbirds are go,
G
A
Thunderbirds are go,
Thunderbirds are,
G
A
G
A
B
Thunderbirds are, Thunderbirds are go.

# *WHAT I GO TO SCHOOL FOR*

*Words and Music by*
*JAMES BOURNE, MATHEW SARGEANT, CHARLIE SIMPSON,*
*JOHN McLAUGHLIN AND STEVE ROBSON*

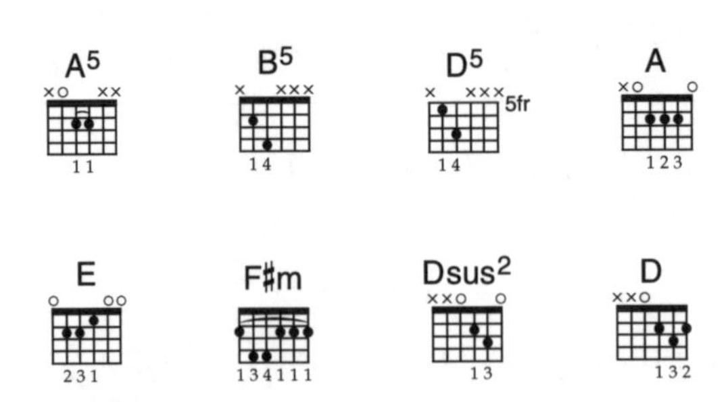


♩ = 200

**Intro**

**Verse 1**

**A** **E**
Her voice is echoed in my mind,
**F♯m** **Dsus2**
I count the days till she is mine.
**A** **E**
I can't tell my friends 'cause they will laugh:
**F♯m** **Dsus2**
I love a member of the staff.
**A** **E**
And I fight my way to front of class
**F♯m** **Dsus2**
To get the best view of her ass;
**A** **E**
I drop a pencil on the floor,
**F♯m** **D**
She bends down and shows me more.

**horus**

```
N.C.          D       A
That's what I go to school for,
                      D
Even though it is a real bore.
                   F#m
You can call me crazy,
                      E
But I know that she craves me.
                      A
That's what I go to school for,
                      D
Even though it is a real bore.
                         F#m
Girlfriends I've had plenty,
                      E
None like Miss Mackenzie.
                      D            E
That's what I go to school for,
N.C.                  A5           B5    D5
That's what I go to school for.
```

**erse 2**

```
A                                E
     So she may be thirty-three
                          F#m       Dsus2
But that doesn't bother      me.
A                                          E
     Her boyfriend's working out of town,
                     F#m          Dsus2
I find a reason to go      round.
A                                     E
     I climb a tree outside her home
                              F#m       Dsus2
To make sure that she's a  -  lone.
A                                E
     I see her in her underwear,
                              F#m         Dsus2
I can't help but stop and       stare.
```

**Chorus 2**

```
N.C.          D       A
That's what I go to school for,
                      D
Even though it is a real bore.
                   F♯m
You can call me crazy,
                      E
But I know that she craves me.
                      A
That's what I go to school for,
                      D
Even though it is a real bore.
                         F♯m
Girlfriends I've had plenty,
                      E
None like Miss Mackenzie.
                      D           E
That's what I go to school for,
N.C.                  F♯m
That's what I go to school for.
```

**Bridge**

```
Everyone that you teach all day knows
       E
You're looking at me in a different way.
D                                      E
   I guess that's why my marks are getting so high.
F♯m
   I can see those tell-tale signs
E
Telling me that I was on your mind.
D
   I could see that you wanted more
                  E                F♯m         E
When you told me that I'm what you go to school for.____
                      D
I'm what you go to school for.
```

**Verse 3**

```
A                                    E
    She's packed her bag, it's in the trunk;
                                F♯m       Dsus2
Looks like she's picked herself a   hunk.
A                                    E
    We drive past school to say goodbye,
                                   F♯m      Dsus2
My friends, they can't believe their   eyes.
```

**Chorus 3**

```
N.C.        D      A
That's what I go to school for,
                   D
Even though it is a real bore.
                F♯m
You can call me crazy,
                   E
But I know that she craves me.
                   A
That's what I go to school for,
                   D
Even though it is a real bore.
                     F♯m
Girlfriends I've had plenty,
                   E
None like Miss Mackenzie.
                   D          E
That's what I go to school for,
N.C.               A
That's what I go to school for. ‖
```

# WHO'S DAVID

Words and Music by
JAMES BOURNE AND TOM FLETCHER

E Asus2 Bsus4 C♯m B A

♩ = 140

**Intro**

```
    E                   Asus2     Bsus4
4/4 ||: / / / / | / / / / | / / / / | / / / / :||
```

**Verse 1**

```
E                                  Asus2
     You've always been this way since high school,
  Bsus4          E
Flirtatious and quite loud.
                              Asus2
I find your sense of humour spiteful,
  Bsus4                C♯m
It shouldn't make you proud.
        B              A                B
And I know your pretty face gets forward guys
C♯m           B            Asus2          B
     But you make it better not to hide the lies.
```

**Chorus**

```
              E              B
Are you sure that you're mine?
               A          B
Aren't you dating other guys?
                    E
'Cause you're so cheap
               B
And I'm not blind.
```

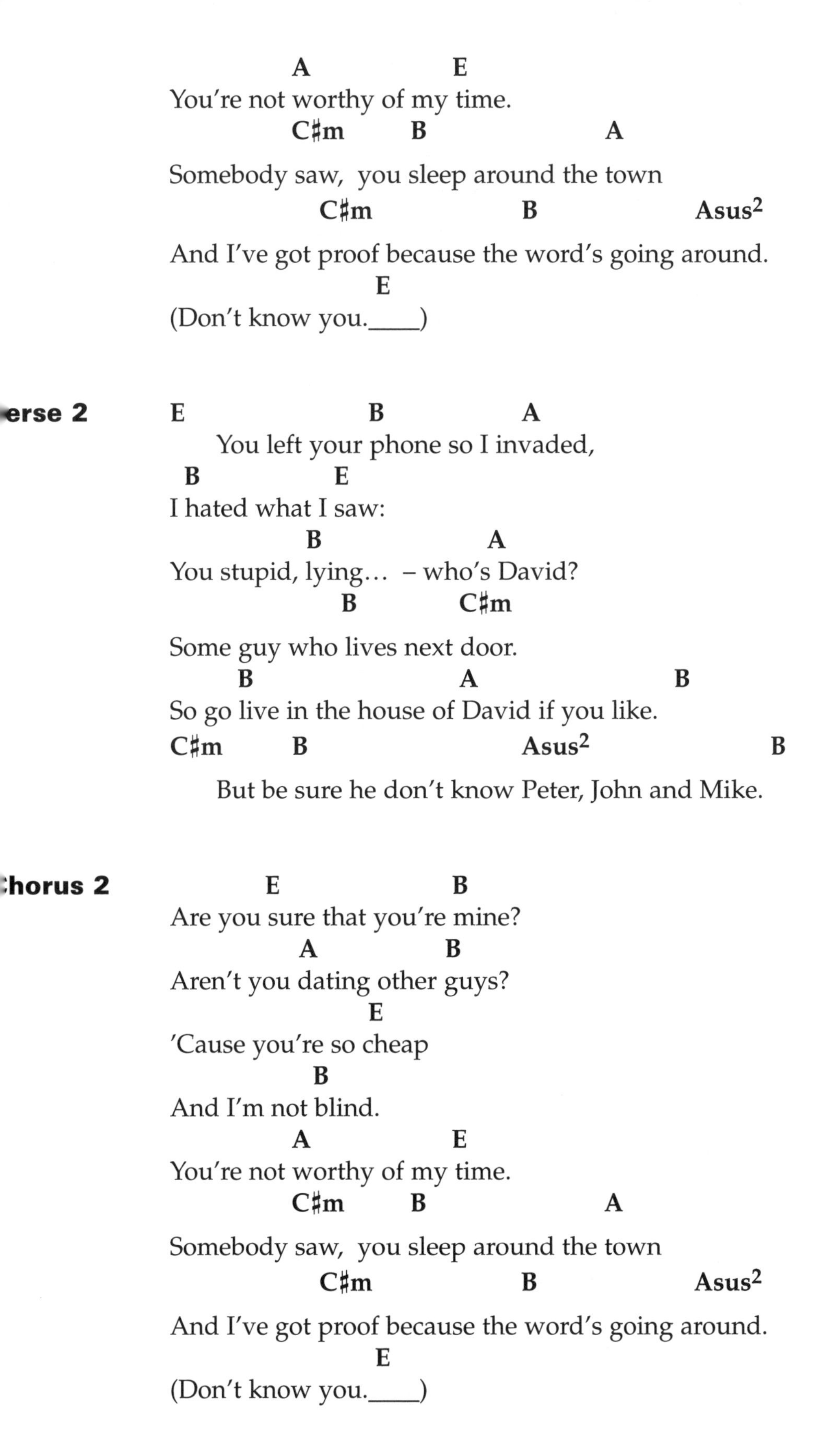

A E
You're not worthy of my time.
C♯m B A
Somebody saw, you sleep around the town
C♯m B Asus2
And I've got proof because the word's going around.
E
(Don't know you.____)

**erse 2**

E B A
You left your phone so I invaded,
B E
I hated what I saw:
B A
You stupid, lying... – who's David?
B C♯m
Some guy who lives next door.
B A B
So go live in the house of David if you like.
C♯m B Asus2 B
But be sure he don't know Peter, John and Mike.

**horus 2**

E B
Are you sure that you're mine?
A B
Aren't you dating other guys?
E
'Cause you're so cheap
B
And I'm not blind.
A E
You're not worthy of my time.
C♯m B A
Somebody saw, you sleep around the town
C♯m B Asus2
And I've got proof because the word's going around.
E
(Don't know you.____)

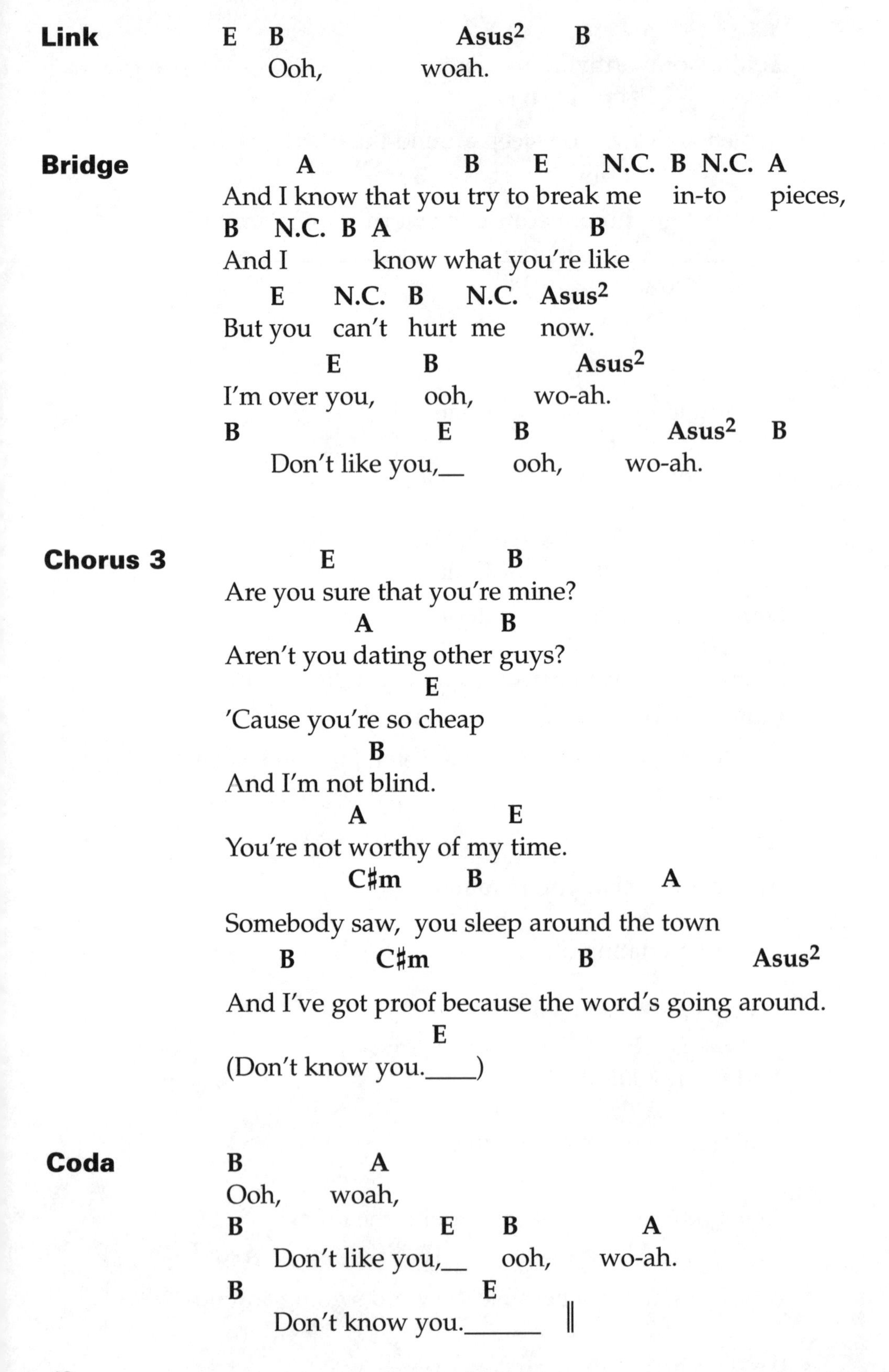

**Link**

**E B Asus2 B**
Ooh, woah.

**Bridge**

**A B E N.C. B N.C. A**
And I know that you try to break me in-to pieces,
**B N.C. B A B**
And I know what you're like
**E N.C. B N.C. Asus2**
But you can't hurt me now.
**E B Asus2**
I'm over you, ooh, wo-ah.
**B E B Asus2 B**
Don't like you,__ ooh, wo-ah.

**Chorus 3**

**E B**
Are you sure that you're mine?
**A B**
Aren't you dating other guys?
**E**
'Cause you're so cheap
**B**
And I'm not blind.
**A E**
You're not worthy of my time.
**C♯m B A**
Somebody saw, you sleep around the town
**B C♯m B Asus2**
And I've got proof because the word's going around.
**E**
(Don't know you.____)

**Coda**

**B A**
Ooh, woah,
**B E B A**
Don't like you,__ ooh, wo-ah.
**B E**
Don't know you.______ ‖

# YOU SAID NO (CRASH AND BURN)

Words and Music by
JAMES BOURNE, MATHEW SARGEANT, CHARLIE SIMPSON,
JOHN McLAUGHLIN AND STEVE ROBSON

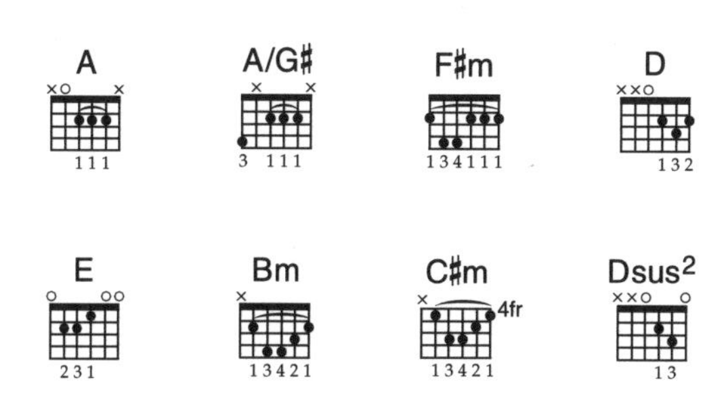


**Capo 2nd fret**

♩ = 180

**tro**
A A/G♯ F♯m D
4/4 | / / / / | / / / / | / / / / | / / / / ||

**erse 1**
A A/G♯ F♯m
You're so fit and you know it,
D E A
And I only dream of you.
A/G♯ F♯m
'Cause my life's such a bitch
Bm C♯m D
But you can change it._____
A E
Maybe you need somebody just like me.
D Bm
Don't turn me down 'cause I've got no car
D
And I've got no money.

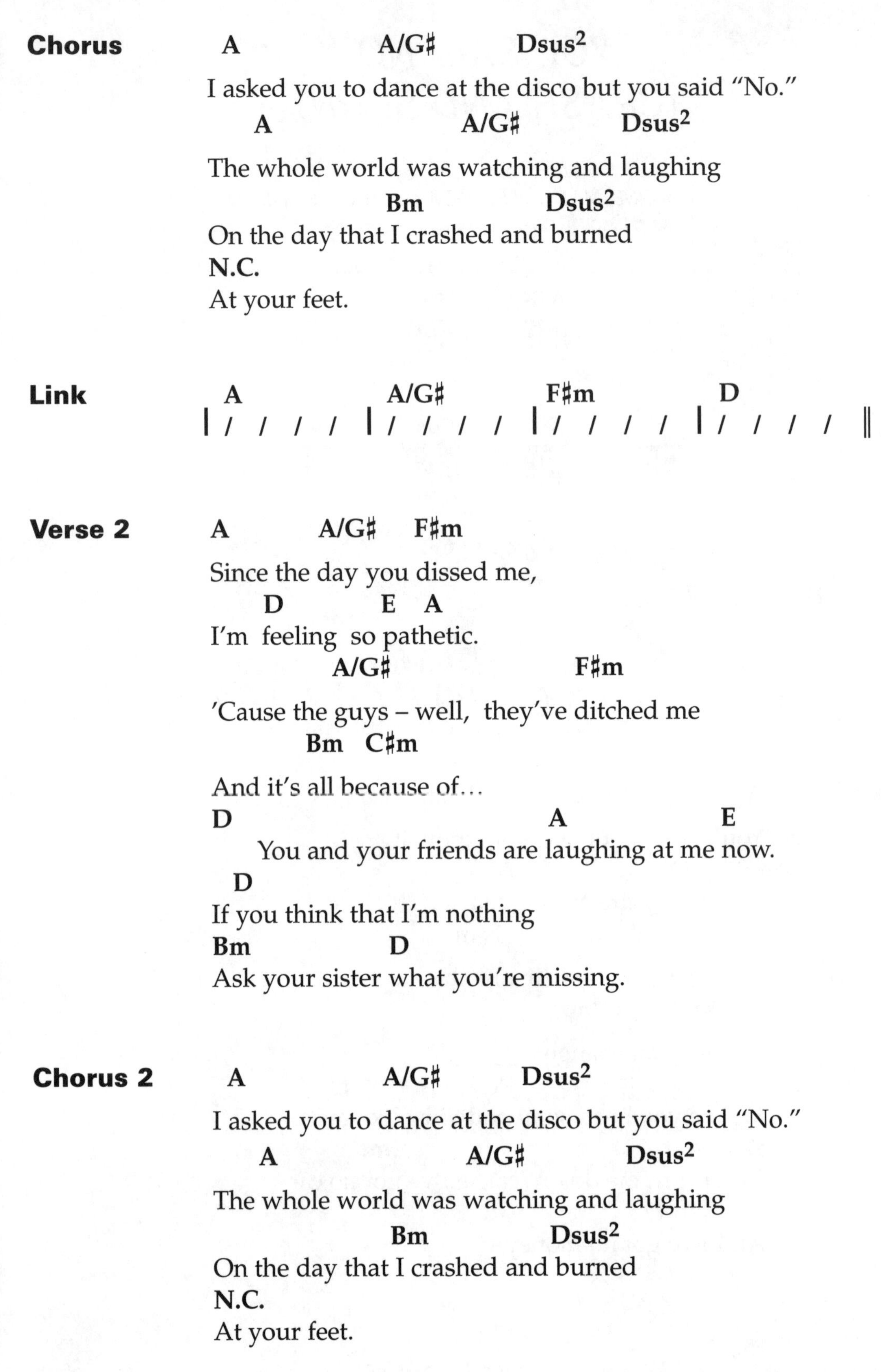

**Chorus**

A A/G♯ Dsus2
I asked you to dance at the disco but you said "No."
A A/G♯ Dsus2
The whole world was watching and laughing
Bm Dsus2
On the day that I crashed and burned
N.C.
At your feet.

**Link**

A A/G♯ F♯m D
| / / / / | / / / / | / / / / | / / / / ||

**Verse 2**

A A/G♯ F♯m
Since the day you dissed me,
D E A
I'm feeling so pathetic.
A/G♯ F♯m
'Cause the guys – well, they've ditched me
Bm C♯m
And it's all because of…
D A E
You and your friends are laughing at me now.
D
If you think that I'm nothing
Bm D
Ask your sister what you're missing.

**Chorus 2**

A A/G♯ Dsus2
I asked you to dance at the disco but you said "No."
A A/G♯ Dsus2
The whole world was watching and laughing
Bm Dsus2
On the day that I crashed and burned
N.C.
At your feet.

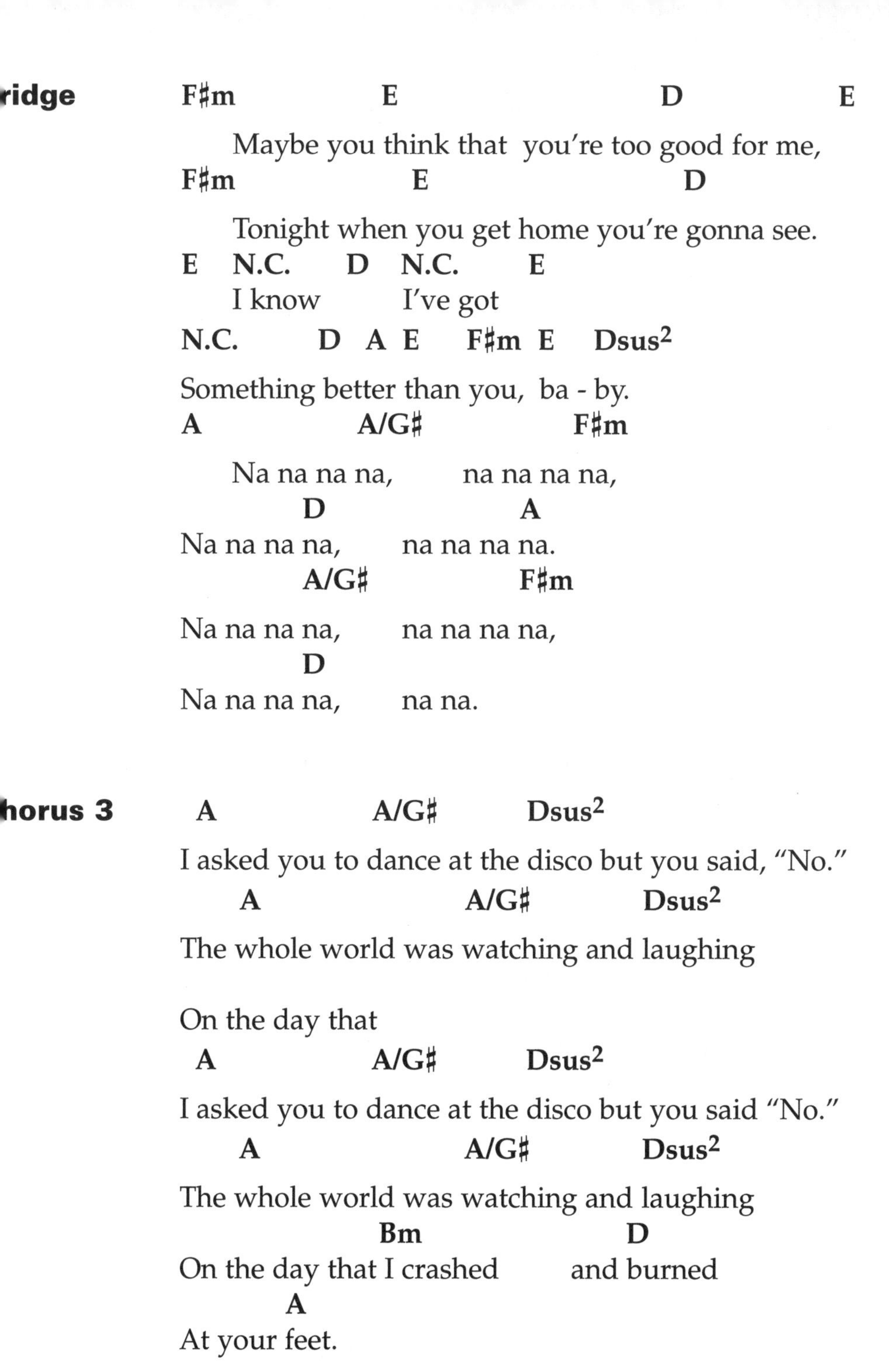

**ridge**

**F♯m E D E**
Maybe you think that you're too good for me,

**F♯m E D**
Tonight when you get home you're gonna see.

**E N.C. D N.C. E**
I know I've got

**N.C. D A E F♯m E Dsus$^{2}$**
Something better than you, ba - by.

**A A/G♯ F♯m**
Na na na na, na na na na,

**D A**
Na na na na, na na na na.

**A/G♯ F♯m**
Na na na na, na na na na,

**D**
Na na na na, na na.

**horus 3**

**A A/G♯ Dsus$^{2}$**
I asked you to dance at the disco but you said, "No."

**A A/G♯ Dsus$^{2}$**
The whole world was watching and laughing

On the day that

**A A/G♯ Dsus$^{2}$**
I asked you to dance at the disco but you said "No."

**A A/G♯ Dsus$^{2}$**
The whole world was watching and laughing

**Bm D**
On the day that I crashed and burned

**A**
At your feet.

# YEAR 3000

*Words and Music by*
*JAMES BOURNE, MATHEW SARGEANT,*
*CHARLIE SIMPSON AND STEVE ROBSON*

A E D F♯m Dsus2 Bm7

**Capo 2nd fret**

♩ = 200

**Intro**

4/4 |: A / / / / | E / / / / | D / / / / | / / / / :| x4

**Verse 1**

A E D
One day when I came home at lunchtime
E
I heard a funny noise:
A E D
Went out to the back yard to find out
E
If it was one of those rowdy boys.
A E D
Stood there was my neighbour called Peter,
E
And a Flux Capacitor.

**Prechorus**

F♯m E
He told me he built a time machine
D
Like the one in a film I've seen, yeah yeah.

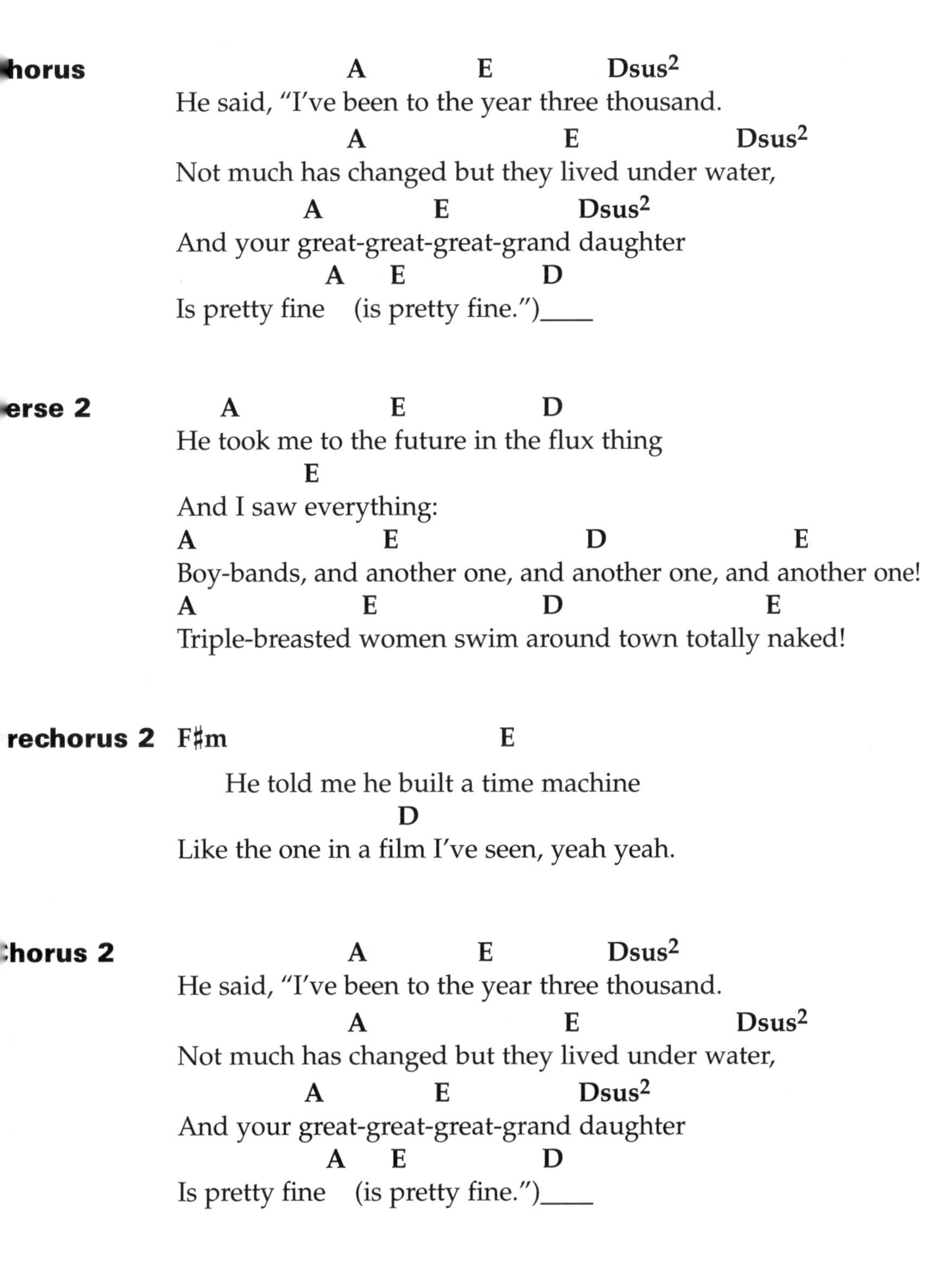

**horus**

A E Dsus2
He said, "I've been to the year three thousand.
A E Dsus2
Not much has changed but they lived under water,
A E Dsus2
And your great-great-great-grand daughter
A E D
Is pretty fine (is pretty fine.")____

**erse 2**

A E D
He took me to the future in the flux thing
E
And I saw everything:
A E D E
Boy-bands, and another one, and another one, and another one!
A E D E
Triple-breasted women swim around town totally naked!

**rechorus 2**

F♯m E
He told me he built a time machine
D
Like the one in a film I've seen, yeah yeah.

**horus 2**

A E Dsus2
He said, "I've been to the year three thousand.
A E Dsus2
Not much has changed but they lived under water,
A E Dsus2
And your great-great-great-grand daughter
A E D
Is pretty fine (is pretty fine.")____

**Bridge**

**A                    E**
I took a trip to the year three thousand:
**D                           E**
This song had gone multi-platinum,
**A                        E**
Everybody bought our seventh album;
**D**
It had out-sold Michael Jackson,
**A                    E**
I took a trip to the year three thousand:
**D                           E**
This song had gone multi-platinum,
**A                        E**
Everybody bought our seventh album,
**D                          E**
(Seventh album, seventh album.)

**Prechorus 3**

**F♯m                           E**
    He told me he built a time machine
**D**
Like the one in a film I've seen, yeah yeah.

**Chorus 3**

**A           E            Dsus$^2$**
He said, "I've been to the year three thousand.
**A                  E              Dsus$^2$**
Not much has changed but they lived under water,
**A          E            Dsus$^2$**
And your great-great-great-grand daughter
**A     E             D**
Is pretty fine    (is pretty fine.")____

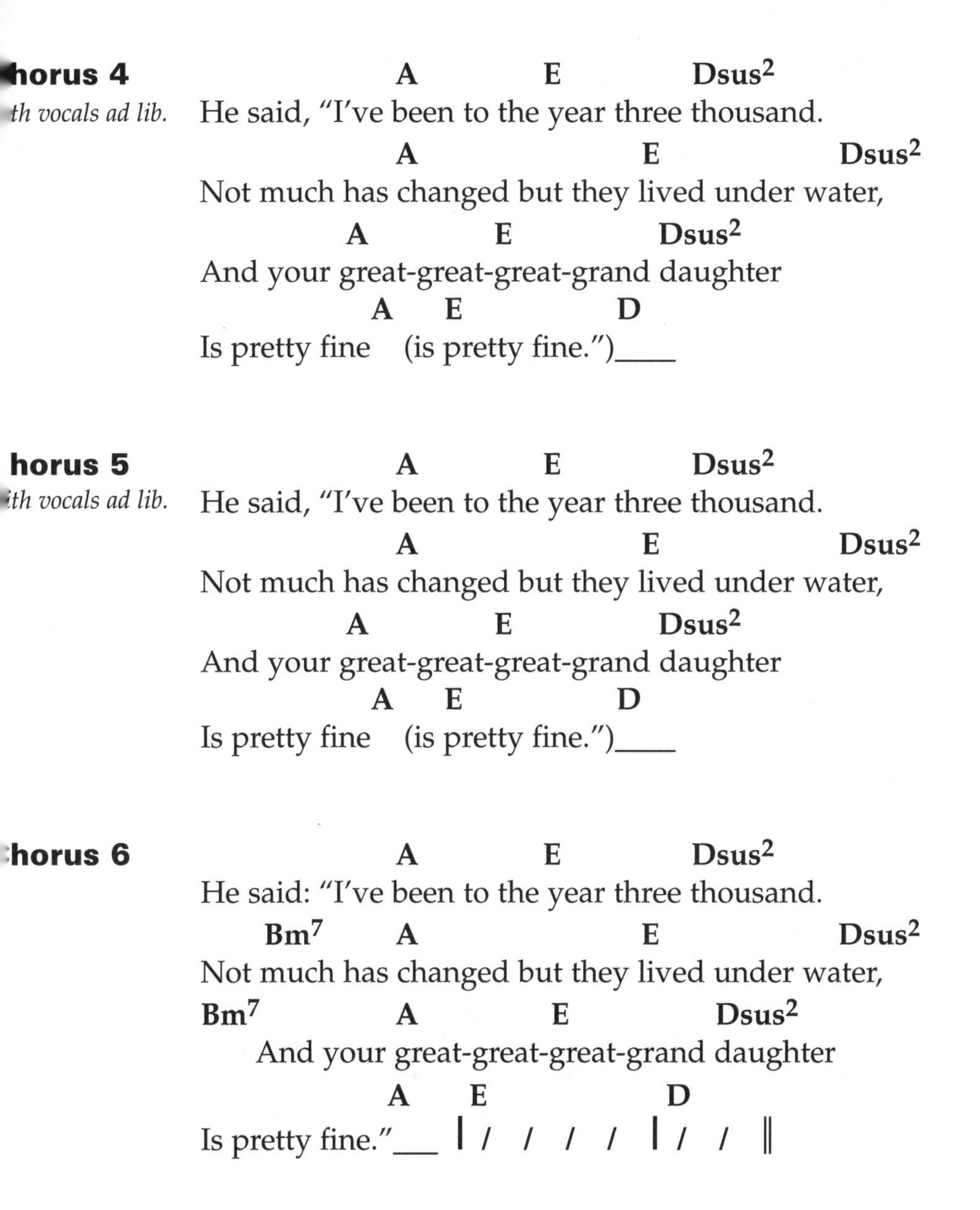

**horus 4**

*th vocals ad lib.*

A E Dsus2
He said, "I've been to the year three thousand.
A E Dsus2
Not much has changed but they lived under water,
A E Dsus2
And your great-great-great-grand daughter
A E D
Is pretty fine (is pretty fine.")____

**horus 5**

*ith vocals ad lib.*

A E Dsus2
He said, "I've been to the year three thousand.
A E Dsus2
Not much has changed but they lived under water,
A E Dsus2
And your great-great-great-grand daughter
A E D
Is pretty fine (is pretty fine.")____

**horus 6**

A E Dsus2
He said: "I've been to the year three thousand.
Bm7 A E Dsus2
Not much has changed but they lived under water,
Bm7 A E Dsus2
And your great-great-great-grand daughter
A E D
Is pretty fine."___ | / / / / | / / ||

# Songs guitars were meant to play

## Essential Acoustic Playlist 2
**9854A VC ISBN: 1-84328-411-1**

A Minha Meninha (The Bees) – Ain't That Enough (Teenage Fanclub) – All Together Now (The Farm) – Alright (Supergrass) – Am I Wrong (Mull Historical Society) – American English (Idlewild) – Average Man (Turin Brakes) – Beetlebum (Blur) – Breakfast at Tiffany's (Deep Blue Something) – Buy It In Bottles (Richard Ashcroft) – Can You Dig It? (The Mock Turtles) – Caught By The River (Doves) – Coffee & TV (Blur) – Come Away With Me (Norah Jones) – Come Back To What You Know (Embrace) – Common People (Pulp) – Crazy Beat (Blur) – Creep (Radiohead) – A Design For Life (Manic Street Preachers) – Distant Sun (Crowded House) – Don't Let Me Down Gently (The Wonderstuff) – Don't Think You're The First (The Coral) – Everlong (Foo Fighters) – Fallen Angel (Elbow) – Fastboy (The Bluetones) – The Final Arrears (Mull Historical Society) – Forget About Tomorrow (Feeder) – Getting Away With It (Electronic) – Go To Sleep (Radiohead) – Grace (Supergrass) – Here's Where The Story Ends (The Sundays) – High And Dry (Radiohead) – History (The Verve) – Hooligan (Embrace) – I Need Direction (Teenage Fanclub) – I Will (Radiohead) – (I'm Gonna) Cry Myself Blind (Primal Scream) – In A Room (Dodgy) – It's True That We Love One Another (The White Stripes) – Just When You're Thinkin' Things Over (The Charlatans) – La Breeze (Simian) – Lilac Wine (Jeff Buckley) – A Little Like You (Grand Drive) – Live In A Hiding Place (Idlewild) – Lucky (Radiohead) – A Man Needs To Be Told (The Charlatans) – No Surprises (Radiohead) – Only Happy When It Rains (Garbage) – Out Of Time (Blur) – Painkiller (Turin Brakes) – Pass It On (The Coral) – Personal Jesus (Johnny Cash) – Pineapple Head (Crowded House) – Poor Misguided Fool (Starsailor) – Road Rage (Catatonia) – Seen The Light (Supergrass) – Seven Nation Army (The White Stripes) – Shine On (The House Of Love) – Silence Is Easy (Starsailor) – Sk8ter Boi (Avril Lavigne) – Stay Away From Me (The Star Spangles) – There There (Radiohead) – Thinking About Tomorrow (Beth Orton) – This Is How It Feels (Inspiral Carpets) – Wake Up Boo! (The Boo Radleys) – Words (Doves) – Yoshimi Battles The Pink Robots (Flaming Lips) – You're So Pretty – We're So Pretty (The Charlatans) – You've Got Her In Your Pocket (The White Stripes)

## Essential Acoustic Playlist
**9701A VC ISBN: 1-84328-207-0**

All The Small Things (Blink 182) – All You Good Good People (Embrace) – Angie (The Rolling Stones) – Any Day Now (Elbow) – Bittersweet Symphony (The Verve) – Buddy (Lemonheads) – Burning Down The House (Talking Heads) – Central Reservation (Beth Orton) – Come Together (Primal Scream) – Cryin' (Aerosmith) – Don't Dream It's Over (Crowded House) – The Drugs Don't Work (The Verve) – Empty At The End (Electric Soft Parade) – Everybody Hurts (R.E.M.) – Everyday Is Like Sunday (Morrissey) – Fast Car (Tracey Chapman) – Fat Lip (Sum 41) – Fell In Love With A Girl (The White Stripes) – Fireworks (Embrace) – Fly Away (Lenny Kravitz) – Future Boy (Turin Brakes) – Going Places (Teenage Fanclub) – Good Riddance (Green Day) – Heaven Knows I'm Miserable Now (The Smiths) – Hotel California (The Eagles) – Hotel Yorba (The White Stripes) – Hunter (Dido) – It's A Shame About Ray (Lemonheads) – Karma Police (Radiohead) – Kiss Me (Sixpence None The Richer) – Losing My Religion (R.E.M.) – Love Burns (Black Rebel Motorcycle Club) – The Man Who Told Everything (Doves) – Mansize Rooster (Supergrass) – Mellow Doubt (Teenage Fanclub) – Movin' On Up (Primal Scream) – Moving (Supergrass) – Mr. Jones (Counting Crows) – Next Year (Foo Fighters) – Novocaine For The Soul (Eels) – Over The Rainbow (Eva Cassidy) – Panic (The Smiths) – Porcelain (Moby) – Pounding (Doves) – Powder Blue (Elbow) – Rhythm & Blues Alibi (Gomez) – Save Tonight (Eagle Eye Cherry) – Silent Sigh (Badly Drawn Boy) – Secret Smile (Semisonic) – Shot Shot (Gomez) – Silent To The Dark (Electric Soft Parade) – Slight Return (The Bluetones) – Soak Up The Sun (Sheryl Crow) – Something In My Eye (Ed Harcourt) – Something To Talk About (Badly Drawn Boy) – Song 2 (Blur) – Song For The Lovers (Richard Ashcroft) – Standing Still (Jewel) – Street Spirit (Fade Out) (Radiohead) – Teenage Dirtbag (Wheatus) – Tender (Blur) – There Goes The Fear (Doves) – Time In A Bottle (Jim Croce) – Underdog (Save Me) (Turin Brakes) – Walking After You (Foo Fighters) – Warning (Green Day) – Waterloo Sunset (The Kinks) – Weather With You (Crowded House) – Wicked Game (Chris Isaak) – Wild Wood (Paul Weller)

## Classic Acoustic Playlist
**9806A VC ISBN: 1-84328-332-8**

Ain't No Sunshine (Bill Withers) – All Tomorrow's Parties (The Velvet Underground) – Alone Again Or (Love) – Another Brick In The Wall Part II (Pink Floyd) – Bad Moon Rising (Creedence Clearwater Revival) – Black Magic Woman (Fleetwood Mac) – Both Sides Now (Joni Mitchell) – Brain Damage/Eclipse (Pink Floyd) – Break On Through (The Doors) – California Dreamin' (The Mamas & The Papas) – Cocaine (Eric Clapton) – Cosmic Dancer (T. Rex) – Crazy Little Thing Called Love (Queen) – Daydream Believer (The Monkees) – Days (The Kinks) – Desperado (The Eagles) – Eight Miles High (The Byrds) – Everybody's Talkin' (Harry Nilsson) – Five Years (David Bowie) – For What It's Worth (Buffalo Springfield) – Fortunate Son (Creedence Clearwater Revival) – Get It On (T. Rex) – Handbags & Gladrags (Rod Stewart) – Happy (The Rolling Stones) – He Ain't Heavy, He's My Brother (The Hollies) – Heroin (The Velvet Underground) – A Horse With No Name (America) – I Feel The Earth Move (Carole King) – It's Only Rock And Roll (The Rolling Stones) – It's Too Late (Carole King) – Itchycoo Park (The Small Faces) – Layla (Eric Clapton) – Leaving On A Jet Plane (John Denver) – Life On Mars (David Bowie) – Light My Fire (The Doors) – London Calling (The Clash) – Long Time Gone (Crosby, Stills & Nash) – Long Train Runnin' (The Doobie Brothers) – The Look Of Love (Dusty Springfield) – Lust For Life (Iggy Pop) – Maggie May (Rod Stewart) – Make Me Smile (Come Up And See Me) (Steve Harley & Cockney Rebel) – Miss You (The Rolling Stones) – Moondance (Van Morrison) – More Than A Feeling (Boston) – Mustang Sally (Wilson Pickett) – New Kid In Town (The Eagles) – Oliver's Army (Elvis Costello) – Pale Blue Eyes (The Velvet Underground) – Perfect Day (Lou Reed) – Silence Is Golden (The Tremeloes) – Sloop John B (The Beach Boys) – Smoke On The Water (Deep Purple) – Space Oddity (David Bowie) – Start Me Up (The Rolling Stones) – Strange Kind Of Woman (Deep Purple) – Stuck In The Middle With You (Stealers Wheel) – Summer In The City (Lovin' Spoonful) – Sunny Afternoon (The Kinks) – Suzanne (Leonard Cohen) – Sweet Home Alabama (Lynyrd Skynyrd) – Tempted (The Squeeze) – Tequila Sunrise (The Eagles) – Turn Turn Turn (The Byrds) – Venus In Furs (The Velvet Underground) – We Gotta Get Out Of This Place (The Animals) – Whiter Shade Of Pale (Procol Harum) – Wuthering Heights (Kate Bush) – You're My Best Friend (Queen) - You've Got A Friend (James Taylor)

## Essential Acoustic Strumalong
**9808A BK/CD ISBN: 1-84328-335-2**

All You Good Good People (Embrace) - American English (Idlewild) – The Drugs Don't Work (The Verve) – Grace (Supergrass) – Handbags And Gladrags (Stereophonics) – Hotel Yorba (The White Stripes) – Karma Police (Radiohead) – Love Burns (Black Rebel Motorcycle Club) – Poor Misguided Fool (Starsailor) – Powder Blue (Elbow) – Silent Sigh (Badly Drawn Boy) – Silent To The Dark (The Electric Soft Parade) – Tender (Blur) – There Goes The Fear (Doves) – Underdog (Save Me) (Turin Brakes)

## Classic Acoustic Strumalong
**9844A BK/CD ISBN: 1-84328-397-2**

Alone Again Or (Love) – Another Brick In The Wall Part II (Pink Floyd) – Cocaine (Eric Clapton) – Get It On (T. Rex) – Handbags And Gladrags (Rod Stewart) – London Calling (The Clash) – Lust For Life (Iggy Pop) – Make Me Smile (Come Up And See Me) (Steve Harley & Cockney Rebel) – Mustang Sally (Wilson Pickett) – Perfect Day (Lou Reed) – Start Me Up (The Rolling Stones) – Stuck In The Middle With You (Stealers Wheel) – Sunny Afternoon (The Kinks) – Venus In Furs (Velvet Underground) – Whiter Shade Of Pale (Procol Harum)

# Available now in all good music shops

A204